Circus

CUS

A World History

Rupert Croft–Cooke
& Peter Cotes

Macmillan Publishing Co., Inc.
New York

Designed by Adina Bartram
and produced by Paul Elek Ltd., London

Macmillan Publishing Co., Inc.
866 Third Avenue, New York, N.Y. 10022

Library of Congress Catalog Card Number: 76-25319

First American Edition 1977

Filmset in England

Printed in France

ISBN 0-236-40051-7 (British ed.)

Half title Circus dog by Mervyn Peake

Contents

Origins of the Circus

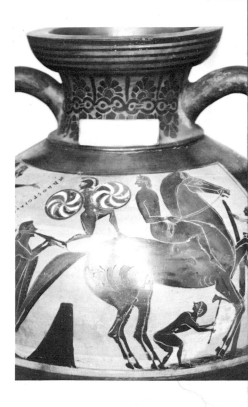

The circus as we know it today owes its origins to Philip Astley, a one-time Sergeant-Major in the 15th Light Dragoons, who gave his exhibitions of equestrian expertise, and later of performing animals, in London in the 1770s. But these can be traced by the historically-minded to similar shows and performances of wild beasts seen in the Circus Maximus and the amphitheatres of Ancient Rome. These in turn were derived from the wondrous exhibitions of exotic animal species and perhaps from chariot-racing in Egypt and Greece.

Philip Astley was not a highly educated man and it is doubtful whether he was fully aware of these fascinating precursors of the art of circus which he founded. Yet the parallel is an interesting one, since in all the centuries between the demise of the Roman circus in the fourth century and the foundation of Astley's Amphitheatre at the end of the eighteenth there was nothing in existence which could properly be called a circus – circus, that is, defined as an organised sequence of performances within a ring of spectators.

There is another curious parallel between exhibitions in the civilisations of the Ancient World and those of Victorian England (and now of Soviet Russia and the United States of America). At particular stages of their history, these empires were at their height. The adoption of the circus as a form of popular entertainment seems to have been stimulated in the heart of a thriving empire, and it may be noted that all circuses provide acts involving foreign animals, in addition to the more usual shows of horsemanship, acrobatics, wire-walking and the rest. In the days when he who was not conquered was a potential enemy, the only certain way in which unusual animals might be procured was through imperial colonists and explorers. Rome, like Greece before it, had established links with India and Persia which facilitated the supply of animals from these countries, just as the establishment of British rule in India made it easy for the followers of Astley to obtain elephants to enrich their shows.

In the same way, as the horizons of these empires were extended, novel species of animals were discovered and the trade routes laid down by which they could be transported to the awe-inspired audiences of London or Rome. The importation of the more exotic life-forms from distant places must have excited the stay-at-home crowds who had never travelled beyond the walls of their native cities, so that circuses have fulfilled the dual purpose of entertaining the public and in rural areas of England educating them in natural history. Shows of foreign animals and their keepers such as those extant in Rome and the cities of Victorian England may well have encouraged an interest in a far-flung empire which otherwise seemed remote to the uneducated masses.

Opposite Spectators watch chariot-racing at the circus; from a Roman mosaic at Gafsa, Tunisia.

Above In this detail from a Greek vase, one acrobat leaps on a horse's back and another shins up a pole.

Opposite top Detail from an Etruscan tomb painting showing a group of entertainers, including one balancing an incense-burner on her head.

Opposite bottom Etruscan fresco painting of a comic dancer wearing a mask.

Overleaf Sophisticated mosaics from a villa in Sicily show how wild animals were captured so that they could be displayed later in the arena in mock hunting displays.

Following page This Roman mosaic at Gafsa, Tunisia, concentrates on chariot racing but also shows a variety of activities within the arena, including the display of wild beasts.

Below A detail from a Greek vase shows a female acrobat performing an elaborate handstand.

Bottom The Persian King, Darius, on a lion hunt. Ambitious expeditions to bring back exotic species of animals, which were then put on public display, first became popular under the Ptolemies.

Finally, the empires of Rome and Great Britain in their heyday were in the process of expansion and innovation. Rich Roman generals and Victorian capitalists encouraged circus entertainments to satisfy the working classes to whom their abundant wealth was in itself a thing of curiosity. Although the Roman prescription of 'bread and circuses' was not consciously employed to keep the masses quiet in early Victorian England, it is possible that without such entertainment to relieve the grim reality of poverty and urban squalor, in the days before the establishment of music-hall, melodrama and those flickering movies that followed the bioscope, they might have been far more ready to pick up revolutionary ideas.

The earliest origins of the Roman circus are to be found in Ancient Egypt. The Ptolemies were a dynasty of Macedonian kings who ruled Egypt from 323 to 30 BC. The first of the line was Alexander the Great's most trusted general, but it is his son, Ptolemy II, who captures the interest of circus historians. By the time he came to rule Egypt, Alexandria was one of the major cultural centres of the Ancient World and this intelligent monarch devoted a large part of his considerable wealth towards the establishment of a magnificent zoological collection. This was gathered from Ethiopia, North Africa, Syria and Northern Arabia, territory acquired through the exploits of the conquering armies of Alexander. Moreover, at Alexandria it became the custom that such exotic beasts should be paraded before the people at important religious festivals. This combined the native Egyptian pageantry with the ritual religious processions of the Greeks. Ptolemy delighted in these displays and his curiosity led him to finance expeditions in search of elephants from Ethiopia, chimpanzees from Africa, and on one occasion a giant snake said to be 45 feet long which was recovered from the marshes of the Upper Nile. It is unclear what species of reptile this could have been, for no snake known today has such proportions, but what is certain is that great skill must have been necessary to transport such a creature alive from the Upper Nile to Alexandria on the coast. The feeding of such animals, then as now, must have been a formidable expense.

One of the most spectacular processions held in Egypt at this time was to mark the festival of Dionysus. This was organised by Ptolemy towards the beginning of his reign. After a representation of Dionysus returning from India, there came twenty-four chariots, each drawn by four elephants; sixty pairs of he-goats drawing chariots; twelve pairs of Saiga antelopes; seven pairs of white oryx, each pulling a chariot; fifteen pairs of hartebeest and eight pairs of ostrich in harness; ass-deer, wild asses, and camels laden with spices; 2,400 hounds from India and elsewhere; one hundred and fifty men carrying trees to which were attached wild animals and birds of all sorts; peacocks, parrots, pheasant and guinea-fowl in cages; unusual breeds of sheep; leopards, panthers, lynxes, a giraffe, a rhinoceros, twenty-four lions of great size and, finally, a

white bear. This last may have been an albino, but it is not impossible that it was actually a polar bear, again demonstrating the ingenuity and skill of the animal hunters of the Greek Empire.

Such a plethora of captive species is very different from the senseless greed for novelty which was later to excite the Romans. Rather it shows an intelligent curiosity and a respectful awe for the wonders of nature. It is small wonder that the Ptolemies are now considered worthy of a place amongst the fathers of science.

When one considers the commercial skill of the Greeks, the broad extent of their empire and their lively curiosity, it is perhaps surprising that Alexandria was the only city able to boast a large collection of exotic animals. Similar menageries were not assembled in the city-states of Greece largely because financial resources were lacking. Yet it was common for the Greeks to keep and make gifts of animals that could be treated as pets or admired for their beauty, and some of these, such as the peacock and monkey, were exotic in origin. They were bred by temples or by private citizens and exhibited by showmen or seen in processions at religious festivals. Greek literature shows close and sympathetic observation of animals and considerable skill in their training. High standards of horse-training and riding were achieved at Sybaris where horses were taught to dance to the sound of the flute. It is hardly conceivable that circus acts should prove decisive in battle but the Sybarites made the mistake of using their equestrian balletomanes for the purpose of war, so that in the conflict between Sybaris and Croton the Crotonites were said to have reduced their opponents' cavalry to a state of dancing confusion by playing appropriate music before the approaching steeds.

In fourth-century Athens Isocrates describes 'men who possess the art of training horses and dogs and most other animals, whereby they make some more spirited and others more gentle and others again intelligent', and 'lions which are more gentle towards their trainers than some men are towards their benefactors, and bears which dance about and wrestle and imitate our skill . . . '

Apart from the 'marvels' given by their trainers, captive wild animals were exhibited in religious processions similar to the celebration of the festival of Dionysus at

Opposite Manuscript illustrations of itinerant medieval performers include a rope-walker, a sword-thrower, a juggler and even a performing bear.

Above This amphora painting, which dates from about 540 BC, shows a chariot being harnessed. Underneath are some of the rare beasts which were paraded at pageants and religious festivals.

Alexandria. These processions were the forerunners of the Roman *pompa*. One of the most important was that in honour of Artemis, the goddess of hunting and wild creatures. In the pageant would be many species, some in cages, some trained to walk quietly beside their handlers, and others in harness. The main feature of this procession was a maiden priestess in a chariot drawn by two stags. This serves to illustrate the advanced state of animal-training in Ancient Greece.

The Greeks had no taste for bloody spectacles, although cock-and-quail fighting was a Greek sport, and bull-fighting was developed in the plains of Thessaly as a demonstration of the skills of the horsemen of this area. In Crete, Minoan bulls were used in a display of acrobatics which had its origins in a religious rite, but when bull-fighting was introduced to Rome in the first century BC, it was swiftly popularised as part of the gory spectacle. The marked disparity in the outlooks of Greece and Rome is well-illustrated by the behaviour of the Seleucid, Antiochus IV, on his return from Rome where he had been held hostage. He had acquired a smear of the Roman taste for blood and almost immediately organised *venationes* (spectacles of the slaughter of wild animals) in Antioch, where nothing of the sort had been seen before. Similarly, after Patrae had been made into a Roman colony by Augustus, (its population being half Italian and half Greek), a new event occurred on the day after the procession of Artemis: boars, stags, roebucks, wolf-cubs and bear-cubs were driven into the flames in brutal Roman fashion. If the animals broke away, they were driven mercilessly back into the fire, and the onlookers declared when the terrified animals did not harm anyone it was a divine miracle. We are more sceptical and believe that the beasts were stupefied by smoke, rather than quietened by supernatural intervention.

In spite of the sharp difference in the attitudes of Greece and Rome to animals, the Romans were undoubtedly influenced by the Greeks and gained much from them in the way of capturing and training wild creatures. In their spectacles the Romans would seem to have combined something of the Greek version of the *pompa* with their own *venatio*, and yet they lost much of the intelligent curiosity which was characteristic of the Greek mentality.

The animal shows of Imperial Rome probably developed from the staged *venatio* of locally-procured wild animals at religious festivals such as the Floralia. During the

Terracotta relief of a Roman charioteer turning the post, always an exciting moment at the Circus Maximus. The emperor Nero was particularly proud of his skill as a charioteer.

Republic there was already a place of exhibition for such shows, the Circus Maximus, although this was built primarily for chariot-racing. Before long an excited lust for bloodshed came to overshadow the Roman spectacle, perhaps because the Romans were very conscious of their image as a martial people and undoubtedly thought it right that they should indulge in such vicious excesses. Having once been introduced, these spectacles came to be demanded by the people and were used as a means to quell their threatened uprisings.

The Circus Maximus in Rome was in the natural declivity between the Palatine and Aventine hills, a valley some 600 or so metres long and 150 broad. Long before any building was constructed for the purpose, chariot races were staged in this almost perfect arena, beside the altar of the god Consus. During the Republic the accommodation for both competitors and spectators was extremely simple. Tarquin the Younger is credited with the erection of the first permanent building, but its rudimentary facilities were not improved until 326 BC when stalls were provided for the horses and chariots.

The two public figures who most clearly illustrate the type of man who used entertainment in the circus for his own political ends during this period of the Republic are Pompey and Julius Caesar. In the later half of the first century BC the aristocracy of the Republic was in decline, and with it the weakly-organised central government of Rome. Before the strongly constituted hub of imperial rule was established by Augustus, there was an unsettled period of transition during which ambitious individuals strode into the arena of public life. In order to enhance their reputations and to increase their share of popularity and acclaim they undertook to entertain the Roman people on a massive scale. The age of the hard-working administrator of the Republic passed into that of the martial leader of the stirring empire. In such an unstable situation, it became necessary for politicians and military generals alike to maintain their rank and strive to improve it. To do so required the support of the masses, a precious and butterfly quantity which would alight on whoever could impress them

A gladiator struggles with a leopard in the arena; from a Roman mosaic.

15

with spectacular entertainments and provide the hungry populace with corn. *Panis et circenses* – bread and circuses – was to remain an imperial maxim for winning the hearts of the Roman people right into the days of the Empire.

In 55 BC, Pompey, a Roman general who had led victorious legions in Spain, Armenia, Syria and Palestine, sought to indulge his mania for power by staging a five-day entertainment of incomparable magnificence. Although he already enjoyed considerable popularity his ambition was to rule Rome without the help of Crassus and Julius Caesar. His plan did not work; but his spectacles must have been the most lavish Rome had ever seen.

The crowd of 150,000 was treated to five days of indulgent extravagance which, in addition to chariot-racing, incorporated several features which would not be altogether out of place in the circus ring today. There were demonstrations of expert horsemanship – riders leapt from one bareback horse to the next; others would ride more than one horse at once, standing astride their backs as they circled the arena at full gallop, a trick such as a contemporary illustration shows one of Astley's riders to perform. Berber jockeys raced camels around the Circus Maximus while others did the same with elephants. Giraffes, then known as 'camelopards', were exhibited before the incredulous audience, as were rarities such as the Gallic lynx, having the shape of a wolf and leopard's spots, a one-horned rhinoceros, probably procured from India via Alexandria, monkeys from Ethiopia, tigers and five hundred Numidian lions and leopards.

Although such displays bore some resemblance to those of Ptolemy in Egypt and more remotely to those of the modern circus, there was an overshadowing dissimilarity. These animals had not been brought to Rome in order to satisfy the people's curiosity about the wonders of Nature and it was not deemed sufficient to parade them before the crowds in a pomp designed to show off their beauty or their oddities. Such was the state

The Colosseum, dedicated by Titus in AD 80. Although it enabled the audience to have a better view of the arena, it held only one fifth as many spectators as did the Circus Maximus and the latter retained its popularity with the Roman crowd: from an engraving by Piranesi.

of mind of the Roman masses at that time that in order to win their approval Pompey sacrificed all these splendid creatures to the mob's lust for blood, a craving only equalled by his own lust for power. And even so his plan misfired. The climax of the proceedings was to be the slaughter of twenty elephants. For once, the mob was not amused. His efforts to win popularity by the killing of these docile beasts aroused not admiration but pity and disgust. For once the Roman delight in cruelty had been over-estimated, and Pompey's horror was not only at his failure as a butcher but at seeing his carefully engineered preparations fall at their climax, bringing down his public image with them.

Julius Caesar, far more intelligent than his political rival, Pompey, was fully aware of the potential of circus entertainment to increase his popularity and used this tool with a confidence which his subordinate lacked. He was a master of crowd psychology and would have been incapable of the disastrous miscalculations of Pompey.

Although he was more interested in gladiatorial combat than in the circus, he was curious in matters of the technical skill which went into staging fights involving horses, elephants, men, and other animals in the arena, and it was he who introduced Thessalian bull-fighting to Rome. He financed much refurbishment of the Circus Maximus, and constructed a moat ten feet wide between the *podium,* the lowest tier of seats, and the arena, as a protective measure towards the spectators when wild beasts were fighting before them. (Nero later filled this in, as by his time all animal fights had been removed to the Colosseum.) Nevertheless, it was not until the foundation of the Roman Empire by the Emperor Augustus, when spectacles became a state monopoly and ceased to be the vehicles of personal advancement, that the building of the Circus Maximus was undertaken with real care and enthusiasm.

Although the derivation of the term 'circus' is a 'ring' or 'circle', the Circus Maximus consisted of tiered seats surrounding a partial ellipse. One end of the ellipse was

Above Gladiators fighting in a Roman amphitheatre. Detail from a mural at Pompeii.

rounded in a continuation of the tiered structure, the other end was straight and at right-angles to the course. This straight end held the main entrance and included the stalls (carceres) for the horses and chariots to be raced. Along the transverse axis of the ellipse ran a fence (spina) in such a way that the starting and return courses were separated. At each end of the course were set three conical pillars (metae) to mark its limits.

Although at the time of Augustus the circus building could not have been very lofty – we know this because it was possible to see the arena from the upper storeys of the houses surrounding the edifice – this emperor expended vast sums upon its fabric. Julius Caesar had rebuilt the chariot stables and cut tiers in the hillside to seat 150,000 people. Augustus largely replaced this crude seating with more lavish structures of stone and marble. To adorn the *spina* between the *metae,* he brought the obelisk of Rameses II from Heliopolis in Egypt and constructed a new imperial box or *pulvinar.* Much of the original circus building had been destroyed by fire in 31 BC, and it is likely that the Augustan restorations were even more extensive than those described.

As well as reconditioning the Circus Maximus, Augustus introduced new species of animals to be exhibited therein. He received many gifts of exotic creatures from African and Asian potentates and was keen to show these to the people. In place of mere slaughter, he encouraged mock hunting scenes to be enacted before the spectators, calculating at the end of his reign that he had supplied 10,000 wild beasts for public shows.

As the Empire expanded even farther, so did the menagerie of the Circus Maximus become more varied. In the sand dunes near Leptis Magna in Tripoli there are some wonderfully preserved relics of this era, the so-called 'Hunting Baths'. The frescoes on their walls recall in vivid detail the hunting and capture of African wild-life for Roman *venationes.* There was undoubtedly a flourishing trade in these beasts from the coast of North Africa to the Italian ports such as Ostia. In the early days of the Empire the majority of animals seen in the arenas of Rome were procured from the hinterlands of North Africa but about the time of Constantine this area was settled and cultivated as cornfields, driving the hunters southward in their quest for game, thus impelling the Roman animal merchants to seek fresh sources. Tigers from India and Persia, bears from Asia Minor, camels, antelopes, wild asses, bison – all these species had been introduced by the end of the first century AD, the public taste for novelty compelling the organisers of spectacles to produce hitherto unknown animals for display.

Elephants were first encountered in the war in Lucania and were introduced to Rome as early as 275 BC, billed under the title of 'Lucanian Oxen'. Over a hundred of these creatures were sacrificed in the circus a couple of decades later and in 99 BC they were made to fight with bulls. Yet they fared better under imperial rule for then they were rarely killed in the Circus and were used instead to pull the imperial chariot or exceptionally heavy loads. Like their counterparts in the Victorian circus, they were

Roman mosaic from Lyons, illustrating the equestrian skills so much admired in Roman times.

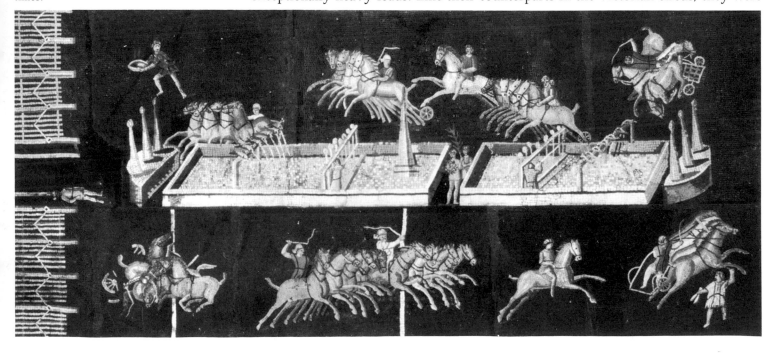

taught to perform tricks, and coins show Roman elephants attired in coats of chain mail probably more decorative than protective.

'African beasts' was a term which came to mean leopards, lions and panthers, and these were seen at the first *venatio* which took place in 186 BC. They became readily available when Rome gained a position of dominance in North Africa but there was an attempt by some of the more conservative statesmen of Rome to forbid their importation into Italy, thus curbing the political power of the *venationes*. This was soon swept aside by the torrent of public opinion and once again animals were allowed to be brought into the country for display in the Circus Maximus. Lions were extremely popular with the circus crowds, particularly if maned, and they were often fought with javelins in the arena.

There were many other animals baited: ostriches were seen at the first *venatio* and later they were chased and shot at with crescent-shaped arrows as they ran. On one occasion three hundred Moorish ostriches were dyed red before being exhibited. Trained cranes were the only other birds to be associated with the spectacles, although brightly-coloured parrots were used to decorate the Forum.

Bears were first exhibited in Rome in the middle of the first century BC but later became numerically more important than African beasts at the spectacles. They came from Numidia, Northern Greece, Spain, Gaul and Germany. Bulls were such a common sight at *venationes* that contemporary writers did not usually bother to enumerate their appearances, but they were set to fight elephants and later men. Boars were also very common but the hippopotamus was a later discovery and rarely seen even in Imperial times.

The crocodile was first brought to Rome by Scaurus who kept five of these creatures, along with a hippopotamus, in a specially constructed reservoir. Augustus flooded the Circus Flaminius and staged a battle in which thirty-six crocodiles were killed, but in another spectacle of the same period men from Tentyra fished them up from the water in nets, let them down again and then swam freely amongst them. Snakes are never mentioned by the Roman historians in connection with the *venationes* and there is only one occasion on which one is recorded to have been shown to the public. They would have proved difficult to display to good effect in the large arena of the Circus Maximus and it is not surprising that larger animals, such as the giraffe and rhinoceros, which could easily be seen and were able to put up a spectacular fight, were more popular.

A mosaic from Gafsa, Tunisia, which captures the atmosphere of circus games.

The Roman methods of catching animals were as varied as those of their capture today. Nets disguised with feathers were used to snare bears, wild boar, deer, wolves and foxes; panthers were caught in traps baited with rotten meat, and hippopotami were trapped in pits. Tigers, once thought to be impossible to catch alive, were hunted by snatching the cubs from their lair. In modern times one circus company possessed its own aeroplane to transport its animals from Africa to England, and there were undoubtedly methods as enterprising which operated to provide adequate supplies of wild beasts to the circuses of Ancient Rome.

When animals were trained, their trainers, or *magistri,* were either slaves or foreigners. It must be assumed that then, as today, they realised that in order to teach an animal to perform a trick it must first be encouraged to enjoy doing so; had they not done so they could not have shown their charges so effectively as they undoubtedly did. Pliny describes trained bulls which, after putting up a mock fight, rolled over and allowed themselves to be caught by their horns. Some of them were even taught to pose as charioteers in specially constructed chariots proceeding at a gallop. Seneca writes of a lion-tamer who placed his hand in the lion's mouth, another who dared to kiss his tiger, and a Negro dwarf who could persuade his elephant to walk a tightrope. Horses, elephants and bulls were trained to perform in water and surprised the first audiences at the Colosseum.

What excited the crowd most was to see an animal perform an unlikely act. For instance, lions which chased hares around the arena only to bring them back unharmed to their trainers were a great favourite with circus audiences, as were leopards which would walk in apparent amity with their natural prey, the antelope, while crocodiles would allow themselves to be ridden by young Egyptian boys.

The Emperor Elagabalus carried this desire to extremes, breaking lions, tigers and stags into harness to draw his imperial chariot. He also delighted in releasing tame lions, bears, and leopards into his guests' bedrooms after they had enjoyed a night's heavy drinking. It says much for the high standard of training at this time that not one of these guests was harmed.

Nevertheless, despite this improvement in the Roman attitude towards animals, they remained a plaything of the people and little intelligent curiosity in them was shown. Perhaps surprisingly it was Nero, that most misrepresented of Emperors, who was one of the few people to stand aloof from the unintelligent Roman disregard for animals. In the grounds of his Golden House at Rome he kept animals of every kind. Largely through his influence the fashion for pets became established and the cat was adopted as a domestic animal.

After the great improvements made by Augustus to the building of the Circus Maximus, the amount of money expended towards its upkeep and modification depended entirely upon the attitude of the Emperor of the time. However, no matter what his personal lack of interest in it might be, no Emperor to succeed to the title had dared to ignore the constant threat from the mob whose power and unruliness increased as the Empire matured. Tiberius, who directly followed Augustus, was virtually the only Emperor who defied the public clamour for spectacles. Otherwise the maxim of 'bread and circuses' was closely observed.

Much of the Circus Maximus was destroyed by fire in the reign of Claudius and this gave him occasion to replace the stone *carceres* (stables) with those of marble and the *metae* of wood with bronze pillars. Nero, his successor, carried out further extensive reconstruction which lasted until the Circus was destroyed by yet another fire during the reign of Domitian, who initiated a programme of rebuilding which was completed by Trajan. The number of *carceres* was increased from eight to twelve and an inscription lauds Trajan as having provided sufficient accommodation in the Circus for the whole population of Rome.

Later restorations of the building are poorly documented but in its final form the Circus Maximus had a seating capacity of between 200,000 and a quarter of a million. The lowest tier of seating was reserved for the senators, the next for the knights, and the remainder for the population at large. Depending upon his social outlook the Emperor sat either with the senators and their families or alone in the imperial box. It was vital for him to maintain the correct balance between excessive aloofness and too common appearance; the proceedings gave him an opportunity to be publicly honoured with applause and stereotyped greetings, these often being set to music. The wiser Emperors manipulated the occasion to gain popularity – to rule and to be seen to rule was an integral part of imperial public relations. However, Marcus Aurelius, who went as far as to be seen reading and signing public documents at the Circus, did not excite respect. When Trajan rebuilt it he thoughtfully discarded the imperial box, realizing he would win approval by sitting amongst the senators. Petitions presented to him there were seldom rejected and one contemporary writer attributes much of the popularity of the Circus to this cause. Moreover, it was one of the few places in Rome where the voice of the public was able to be heard. There were no public meetings to discuss political issues and for some reason the unrestrained outbursts of the crowd in the theatre and circus were tolerated to a degree which was unknown elsewhere. Later this theatre of democracy became abused as public ridicule of both Emperor and Senate was freely expressed. 'Safety in numbers' ensured that complainants were difficult to punish, and a tolerant attitude increased an Emperor's popularity.

Although the Circus Maximus was the only place of public entertainment where there was no segregation of the sexes, the early Emperors strictly regulated the dress of those who attended its performances. Even in high summer Roman citizens were compelled to wear togas, a burden which often spoiled their pleasure. One example of the rigid social discipline of the time is to be found during the reign of Domitian, when in the middle of a spectacle there broke a heavy storm which showed no sign of ceasing. The Emperor carefully cloaked himself against the elements, but would not allow the spectators to move from their places. Unprotected from the storm many fell ill and died from this enforced loyalty. The same Emperor declined to allow the wearing of any coloured dress in the Circus with the exception of white, scarlet and purple. The seriousness with which this edict was regarded says much for the importance of the Circus in Roman society at this time. Augustus allowed people to enter the Circus barefoot in summer but Tiberius later revoked this liberty.

In AD 80 Titus, dedicating the Colosseum, pronounced that it be advertised as 'The World's Greatest Amphitheatre'. Yet its seating capacity was five times smaller than that of the Circus and although people could obtain a clearer view of the proceedings the Circus remained the favourite resort of Romans.

In AD 100 Pliny the Younger wrote of the Circus that its endless length (1,875 feet) was in harmony with the gorgeousness of its temples; it was worthy of the sovereign nation and in itself was no less remarkable than the games exhibited in it. The decorations were rich throughout and the seats were embellished with bronze. The three-storey Circus was surrounded by a single-storey building which had entrances and exits capable of dealing with the flow of thousands of people at once. In the cellars of this structure were housed shops, lavatories and the entrances, while the owners lived up above. Astrologers plied their trade in these precincts. As the festival days approached there was much betting and consultation of soothsayers in connection with the chariot-racing. Tablets of lead were laid in graves and demons were conjured up to injure or delay a particular charioteer. Amulets, carrying the image of Alexander the Great, were sold in the forecourts of the circus to ward off accidents and avert danger from the favourites.

It was in this industrious annexe of the Circus Maximus that most of the numerous fires had their origin. There were many shops where food was cooked to feed the massed spectators and brothels were there to satisfy other needs. 'The road to the Circus lay through the brothel,' as one latterday Christian writer has remarked. The prostitutes, many of whom were girls from the Near East, danced in oriental dress to the sound of drums, cymbals and castanets.

In the empty arena the principal object of interest must have been the *spina*, the ornate fence which bisected the course. The great Egyptian obelisk brought to the Circus by Augustus was dwarfed by an even larger one obtained by Constantius. In addition to these there were decorated shrines and images set along the *spina*, as well as seven figures of dolphins and seven oval objects, one of which was removed as each lap of a race was completed.

Chariot races and acts involving trained animals were held on the final day of public festivals. At the time of the Republic there were seven of these which came to occupy sixty-six days. The Roman Games took up fifteen (4–19 September); the Plebeian Games fourteen (4–17 November); those of Ceres eight (12–19 April); the Festival of Apollo eight (6–13 July); that of the Great Mother eight (3–10 April); the Floralia took place on six days from 28 April to 3 May; and the Sullan Commemoration occupied seven days

from 26 October to 1 November. Of these sixty-six days fourteen were devoted to the races, two to trials of racehorses, two to sacrifices and forty-eight to theatricals, but the races were most popular. All these festivals except the last existed in some form or other until the fourth century. After the fall of the Republic various Emperors added further festivals but the number was variable especially as their total was increased by triumphs, dedications and imperial birthdays. Most rulers sought to extend the public holidays – Nerva and Severus were almost unique in their pruning of the games for economic reasons – and by the middle of the fourth century there were no less than 175 days of festival, sixty-four in the Circus, 101 in the theatre, and the remainder devoted to gladiatorial combat. When the Flavian Amphitheatre, the Colosseum, was dedicated in AD 80, there was a 100-day festival in commemoration of the event.

Although gladiatorial combat stole some of the popularity of the Circus, the chariot races in the Circus Maximus remained a very important part of the festivals. The seats were always occupied before dawn and it is recorded that the excited noise of the crowd on its way to the Circus disturbed the sleep of at least two Emperors – Caligula sent soldiers out to cudgel the masses into silence, the nobility and poor perishing alike, and Elagabalus threw snakes into the crowd causing a terror in which many were trampled to death. For reasons of safety most noblemen were carried through the throng by two sturdy slaves.

A religious ceremony preceded the races. Down from the Capitol came a great procession with either the Emperor or the benefactor of the games at its head. If the latter, he would be bedecked in the costume of a triumphant general – a gold-braided toga of purple, a tunic embroidered with palms, an ivory sceptre adorned with the head of an eagle carried in his hand and a slave holding a huge wreath of golden oak leaves set with jewels above his head. His children sat with him and he was preceded by a band of musicians. As his entourage of white-robed citizens entered the gates of the Circus Maximus they were heralded by the sounds of flute and trumpet. In mule-drawn carts following the president of the ceremony came statues of the gods accompanied by priests. There was a great deal of religious ceremony attached to the procession and the ritual had to be carried out perfectly, or else repeated.

When all was ready and the Emperor had been revered, the president of the games leant from his balcony and dropped a white flag onto the course. At this signal – a sign of Lucifer to the early Christians – the first race began. Each race consisted of seven laps of the course, a total distance of eight kilometres. The chariots started abreast, but in an oblique line so that the outer vehicles were compensated for the greater circumference of their paths. There would be up to twenty-four of these races or *missi* in a single day but after one race the air was so thick with dust that the course had to be watered to settle it. This added to the confusion, danger and excitement. The crowds grew ecstatic in their shouts of encouragement and were hysterical in their jubilation when a favourite won. The charioteers, drawn mainly from freedmen or slaves, were fully aware of the dangers of their profession and used every guile they knew to gain a few metres on their opponents. The most effective method was to force all others to overturn, but each driver carried a knife with which to cut himself free should this happen to him. The savage exultation of the crowds and the grim determination of the hardened charioteers clearly indicate that this was a sport tinged with the madness of a cult.

Yet the cries of the crowd were directed neither towards individual horses nor, in most cases, towards specific drivers. Competition was between the four companies (*factiones*) of chariots denoted by their house colours of red (*russata*), white (*albata*), green (*prasina*) and blue (*veneta*). Two more, purple and gold, were added by Domitian but fell into disuse after his death. The *factiones* came into being when the racing business grew too large for the individual charioteers to organise for themselves and they were managed by capitalists and rich stud-owners. The benefactors of the races then contracted horses, drivers and chariots from the faction managers. Great care was devoted to training the horses and these were selected principally from Spain, Syria and Cappadocia in Turkey. In the early Empire African horses of Spanish blood were reputed to make the best racehorses.

Chariot-racing supported a whole community of skilled workmen who populated the stables of the *factiones* located near the Circus Flaminius. These were grooms, artisans, artists, officials, wheelwrights, shoemakers, tailors, pearl-workers, physicians, instructors, messengers, runners and cellarers, mainly drawn from the lower orders of society.

Opposite Exotic animals were displayed in processions at festivals such as in the one in honour of Dionysus, shown here. Camels and leopards were amongst the animals which dazzled the Roman spectators.

23

The circus *factiones* of Rome and Constantinople were among the most remarkable phenomena of the Empire. The whole population from the Emperor to the humblest slave was divided into four hostile camps, later reduced to two. The Emperors not only encouraged their favourite faction but incited violence and terrorized all opposition. Even those who had no real interest in the racing itself adopted a colour and everything else was subordinated to this passion. In Constantinople, in the middle of the fourth century, the factions became intermingled with politics and religion, and rioting broke out. References to this social evil in Rome are few but there is no reason to suppose that it was any less intense than that in the Eastern capital. A few isolated instances of this excess zeal stand out: at the funeral of a red charioteer one of his supporters threw himself upon the pyre, and as late as the third century Caracalla shamelessly drove his chariot on to the course, and upon hearing an outcry against his faction, the blues, ordered the offender to be executed. In this strained atmosphere petty quarrels were exaggerated into national feuds; and this sort of rivalry survived the Western Empire and died out only when the Circus finally vanished. The last race was held in the deserted ruins of Rome in 549 under Totila the Goth. But some would say the spirit of its organisation still lingers on in the Palio, held in the great piazza of Siena every year.

It is hardly surprising that the cult of chariot-racing came to absorb much of the arena-time in the Circus Maximus and grew to frenzied proportions in the minds of the Roman people. It was a great social leveller and it was common for all young nobles to ride and carry out the stable chores themselves. The horse-goddess Epona was highly revered and several Emperors mastered the art of the charioteer, among them Caligula and Nero. Others preferred merely to select their young favourites from among the heroes of the racecourse.

However, apart from the two, three and four-horsed chariot races skilled horsemen began to entertain the circus crowds in more novel ways. In one variation riders would command two horses at once, jumping from one to the other during the race. Such contests were known as *desultores* and have already been described here as forerunners of Astley's entertainments.

One writer describes the racehorses as being encouraged by flutes, dances, coloured ribbons and flaming torches. Such a description is highly evocative of the bright lights, the band and the gaiety of the circus as we know it today. Yet in the huge arena surrounded by a quarter of a million shouting spectators it is unlikely that the music was audible to anyone except perhaps the horses for whom it was played.

Apart from acts involving horses there arose many varied demonstrations which pleased the audiences of Rome as much as they do those of today. Even before the onset of imperial rule Rome copied the Greek and Etruscan ideas, though Greek athletic contests were forbidden in the circus ring, as the Romans, less clean-minded than the Greeks, considered that the sight of naked runners was indecent. But at the major festivals there were fireworks, rope-dancers, jugglers, acrobats and boys turning somersaults. Pliny describes a giant who walked across the stage bearing armour and shoes weighing a colossal 1,000 Roman pounds.

Decorations on the colonnade of a stable in the Palatium have given us a picture of these varied sideshows: a rope-dancer is seen dancing with buskins on thin, almost invisible ropes; a wall-climber teases a bear and then clambers up a sheer precipice to make his escape; bears and bands of hundreds of flutes, trumpets and other wind instruments, perform as do a thousand athletes and actors with masks. The stage was provided with transformation scenery and the poet Claudian describes an exhibition in which there were chariot races, athletic contests, animal baitings, theatricals and music. Acrobats were said to fly like birds and they formed human pyramids with a boy crowning the top exactly as acrobatic teams do today. The Romans were skilled in pyrotechnics and there were feats involving harmless flames. There were scenes to inspire wonder and one writer speaks of 'men who hovered in mid-air whilst others jumped to the ground from a scaffolding, leaping through fire, soaring like dolphins in space, as unfeathered birds'.

As many of the festivals, such as the Floralia, were held in the evening or during the night, artificial light was supplied and the forum and *comitium* were illuminated by lamps, partly decorative and partly functional. The secular games of Augustus by custom lasted throughout the night, young boys and girls being refused admission unless accompanied by their parents. Objections on the grounds of morality were successfully countered with reassurances that the lights would be too bright, and

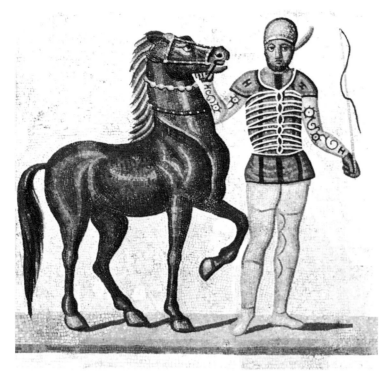

perhaps the splendour of the illuminations became an end in itself. One is inevitably reminded of Christians soaked in pitch, said to be used by Nero to provide light for one of his nocturnal revels.

Feasting was another important feature at the Circus. At midday there was a break for luncheon when slaves brought baskets of food and wine to their masters. At the greater festivals a whole day and night might be set aside for a feast and in AD 88 on the festival of 1 December the youngest and most beautiful of imperial slaves were selected to attend to the wants of the spectators, whose number they equalled. They were dressed in rich costume and circulated among the crowd showering imperial gifts of food and wine on them with no regard for class – on this occasion the poor man fared as well as the senator. Tickets for prizes were also included in the shower of bounty and these entertainments were so popular that special patrols had to guard the deserted streets from looting. People of all nations flocked to pay tribute to the Emperor at such festivals – and to relieve him of his gifts.

Mosaic showing the four 'factiones' of Rome. These rival groups, each sporting a different colour, were originally formed for competitive chariot racing. They quickly became involved, however, in political and religious disputes, drawing their supporters from all sectors of the population.

It remains to note that the Circus Maximus and the Colosseum were not the only forerunners of the modern circus in the Roman Empire. Of secondary importance in Rome was the Circus Flaminius, built in 221 BC but not mentioned after the first century. Caligula erected the Circus Neronis in the gardens of Agrippina, its dubious excesses gaining widespread notoriety. Another was constructed by Maxentius outside the Porta Appia, where its ruins may still be seen.

With the advance of the Empire other Roman amphitheatres were erected at Verona, Capua and Pompeii in Italy; at the port of Syracuse in Sicily; at Tarragona and other cities in Spain; at Arles, Nîmes and Bordeaux in France; and at Silchester and Cirencester in England. In almost one hundred places of entertainment, audiences were thrilled by fights between men and wild animals and astounded by daring feats of equestrianism and acrobatics. Chariot-racing lasted until the end and when the Goths had occupied the ruined city of Rome the last show in the Circus Maximus flickered before a disenchanted audience, as the last lights of a once-glorious empire were extinguished and Europe slid into the gloom of the Dark Ages. With the collapse of the complex society which had produced them, most of these buildings in common with the Circus Maximus and Colosseum fell into disuse and ultimately served as quarries for the builders of succeeding generations.

If the Roman *venationes* seem quite alien to our understanding of circus, we should turn to a newspaper of 1932 which describes boar and stag hunts taking place in Paris.

A new era has opened for the world enclosed within the circle of the circus ring with two new productions that are attracting large audiences to the two Paris circuses, the Cirque Medrano, founded by the famous clown 'Boum Boum', and the Cirque d'Hiver.
Trapeze artists, jugglers and the old-time foolers have given place to spectacular shows such as have never been produced in any enclosed theatre before.
At the Cirque d'Hiver there are staged a boar-hunt and a stag-hunt complete with wild boars and stags. The old blaring selections by the circus orchestra have been superseded

Gladiatorial combat between men and wild animals was a popular spectacle which satisfied the Roman lust for bloodthirsty sport. This eighteenth-century print conveys the chaos and horror of such events.

by hunting calls on the big circular horns carried by the servants of the French hunts. All the scenes of the hunt, which closely resemble those familiar to foxhound followers in England, are portrayed as faithfully as possible, the spectacle working up with a pack dashing across the ring to the kill.

It must not be supposed that after the fall of the Roman Empire in the fourth century AD the acts that had been popular among its circus-loving people vanished entirely, but it is a fact that nothing at all resembling the Circus Maximus and its displays was assembled anywhere in the world until the end of the eighteenth century in England. Authorities on what we now call 'the circus' in fact deny that any real relationship can be established between the Circus Maximus of Rome and Astley's Amphitheatre in London, but it is a vital part of the thesis of this book that although there were fundamental differences in spirit, training and display, the two are related by more than their names and a rope-walker in Rome, for instance, and even perhaps a charioteer would recognize his descendants today.

But to establish any distinct connection between the two is more difficult. Horsemanship, of course, continued to be practised through the centuries in many forms, while acrobats, clowns, bear-leaders, animal trainers, jugglers and tumblers wandered about Europe avoiding the most dangerous trouble-centres and earning a few groats by their exhibitions on fairgrounds or in the street, but no centre for such arts, no place of exhibition existed and no organised displays were encouraged.

A few gaping peasants watched the skilled acrobats whose fathers had thrilled the Roman populace; a scruffy bear-leader who had slept in a barn with the animal he showed persuaded the mangy creature to waddle round while children watched fearfully; but although the high-born warriors practised for their tournaments and *caballeria* there were no leaping riders or charioteers to please the common people. The nearest thing to a circus ring for many centuries was the rough circle formed by a group of curious onlookers when an itinerant juggler or tumbler showed his prowess on a village green.

As for the amphitheatres, which had been built not only in the Roman cities but in towns in their furthest colonies, these fell into decay like the Colosseum itself, except in some Spanish cities where they were reconstructed and turned to the purposes of bull-fighting, which we will notice later as a bastard offshoot of the Roman Circus.

So even if we recognize the Circus Maximus as the forerunner of the Ring which Philip Astley enclosed on a piece of wasteland called 'Ha'penny Hatch' in Lambeth in 1768, it is no easy matter to account for a gap of fourteen centuries during which nothing that could be recognized as a circus in either the ancient or the modern sense of the term existed. If even one large troupe of acrobatic or animal-training performers had set up their pitch outside or in a European centre of population in, say, Renaissance times or the Age of Discovery of the New World, one could argue that the circus had never died; but no such phenomenon is recorded or described in history or folklore. The medieval itinerant showman seems to have been a lonely creature, whom we see travelling the road with a pack, a packhorse or a performing animal who earned a living

Medieval animal feats were less spectacular than Roman ones, but bear-baiting and cock-fighting were popular and travelling showmen successfully trained animals to perform balancing tricks.

for him; or later as one of a band of waggoners with their tents and trappings carried from fair-ground to fair-ground, from castle to barn. Sometimes the rear of such a wagon would open to make a stage for the jugglers, conjurers, ballad-singer or buffoon to perform on. But it was a desperate sort of life and by the sixteenth century Philip Stubbes, speaking for his respectable contemporaries, saw in such performers the personification of all vices, and he justifies in violent terms his contempt for 'suche drunken sockets and bawdye parasits as range the cuntreyes, ryming and singing of vncleane, corrupt and filthie songes in tauernes, ale-houses, innes, and other publique assemblies'.

One possible link between the two epochs of the circus might be the bands of wandering gypsies who appeared in Europe in the fourteenth century and in Britain some century or more later. They have been used by romantic-minded historians as evidence for so many far-fetched theories that it is perhaps disappointing to find that for this one there is not the least tittle of argument; indeed there are clear and decisive negatives at every turn. The gypsies came from India, as the remains of their language testify without any doubt, and their arts were oriental – metalwork, fortune-telling, music and dance. They were skilled in horse-breaking and riding but they used horses as other itinerant people did, to carry themselves and their belongings from place to place. They danced and made music for their own pleasure and although it may be that in the nineteenth century the gypsies as fellow wayfarers and horsemen were recruited into the ranks of showmen, and perhaps even sometimes of circus performers, there is no reason to suppose that this had anything to do with their way of life or origins. All that they had in common with the folk who practised some of the arts of the old circus was their itinerancy. Their popular name was derived from 'Egyptian', and some fanciful theorists have seen a clue in this, especially as one of their early leaders called himself 'Lord and Earl of Little Egypt'. But this was a red herring. They were called Egyptians because they were swarthy and it was vaguely supposed that such people came from Egypt.

But the origins of one spectacle, popular in Spain in one guise or another for two thousand years, was certainly seen in different forms in Imperial Rome, though it seems to have been imported from the Iberian Peninsula first by Julius Caesar. That, of course, was the bull-fight, or more correctly and anciently the Bull-Running – the *corrida de toros*.

That it quickly became popular is shown by Suetonius who writes: 'Between the years 41-45 AD, Tiberius Claudius produced spectacles of wild animal baiting, Trojan games, and African hunts executed by Praetorian horsemen led by their Tribunes with their Prefect amongst them. He presented the Thessalian horsemen who give chase to bulls in the Circus until, tiring them, they leap on their backs and taking firm hold of the horns, twist their necks and bring them down [known in U.S. rodeos as 'bulldogging'],and also the Iberians who use their skins or cloaks to avoid the repeated attacks of their savage bulls before killing them.' Popular demand also led Augustus to build the Statilus Taurus which, as the name implies, was the first Roman amphitheatre designed expressly for the imported Iberian spectacle known as *taurilia,* which gradually degenerated into sacrificing criminals and Christians to wild beasts.

It may well be that the amphitheatres in various parts of Spain, left derelict and crumbling, encouraged bull fighting. Certainly Roman amphitheatres at Seville,

Above and opposite In the Middle Ages groups of itinerant performers travelled all over the country and entertained the villagers with feats of tumbling and juggling.

Above left An Anglo-Saxon juggler performing to music.

Top left A horse beating a tabor, a trick performed in the Middle Ages

Right A jester amuses a group of noblemen with his jokes and antics in an illuminated capital of a fifteenth-century manuscript.

Below A sixteenth-century engraving showing hoop-jumpers.

Cordoba, Segovia, Toledo, Tarragona, Merida and Cadiz were rebuilt and refurbished and some of them serve as bull-rings to this day.

Tell a modern circus performer that his exhibition has, or ever has had, anything in common with the Spanish bullfight and he would probably be extremely angry, because in a notable respect one is the exact antithesis of the other – performing animals in the circus are reputedly trained by infinite patience, understanding and kindness, whereas the bull in the Spanish *corrida* must be killed – with skill, with art, with courage, but finally and inescapably. Bull-fighting is the conflicting offshoot of one not very important aspect of the Roman circus, but it has too many similarities in procedure, in the arenas in which it is shown and in the kind of excitement it provokes to deny its common origin with the savage exhibitions in the Circus Maximus. It may be because of the Spanish climate in the bull-fighting season, it may be because of the ring itself with its stone seats, or it may be because of the complexion and noise of the crowd of Mediterranean people, but certainly with a little effort one can imagine oneself, not in the *sombra* seats of a newly erected *plaza de toros,* but in a Roman amphitheatre in the time of the indulgent Emperors.

Left A group of jesters wearing the traditional cap and bells perform a dance: from a thirteenth-century manuscript.

Below In this seventeenth-century German engraving a troupe of rope-walkers entertain the crowd at a fencing school in Nuremberg.

However, this parallel is at best a diversion into a blind alley and impedes our attempt to trace the history of the circus as we know it today.

But there were more presages of the circus to come. In particular the rope-walkers followed a direct tradition from the rope-walkers of Rome and it is interesting to find them exhibiting their acts before there was anything in the modern world which could properly be called a circus. There were for instance the Ravels, of whom there are records dating from 1603; the Chiarinis; the Wallendas and the Knies. It was Jean Ravel, called Blondin, who gave his name to his apprentice, the famous Blondin whose real name was Emile Gravelet. But rope-walkers were in great favour during the seventeenth and eighteenth centuries, when every fair had one of these performers, each claiming to be more sensational than any rival.

On 13 September, 1660, John Evelyn noted in his diary:

'I saw in Southwark, at St Margaret's Faire, monkies and asses dance and do other feats of activity on ye tight rope; they were gallantly clad *à la mode,* went upright, saluted the company, bowing and pulling off their hatts; they saluted one another with as good a grace as if instructed by a dancing master. They turned heels over heads with a basket having eggs in it, without breaking any; also with lighted candles in their hands and on their heads, without extinguishing them, and with vessells of water, without spilling a drop. I also saw an Italian wench dance and performe all the tricks on ye tight rope to admiration; all the court went to see her.'

Eight years later, on 21 September, Pepys was industriously recording:

'To Southwark Fair, very dirty, and there saw . . . Jacob Hall's dancing on the rope, where I saw such action as I never saw before, and mightily worth seeing; and here took

Opposite Amongst the crowds at Southwark Fair a rope-walker can be seen performing. The tradition of rope-walking was one of the direct links between the circus of Rome and the modern circus; from an engraving of Southwark Fair after Hogarth.

Below A talented monkey performs at Sadlers Wells. The trainer is Signor Spinacuta who later went to Philadelphia with John Bill Ricketts and became one of the pioneers of the American circus.

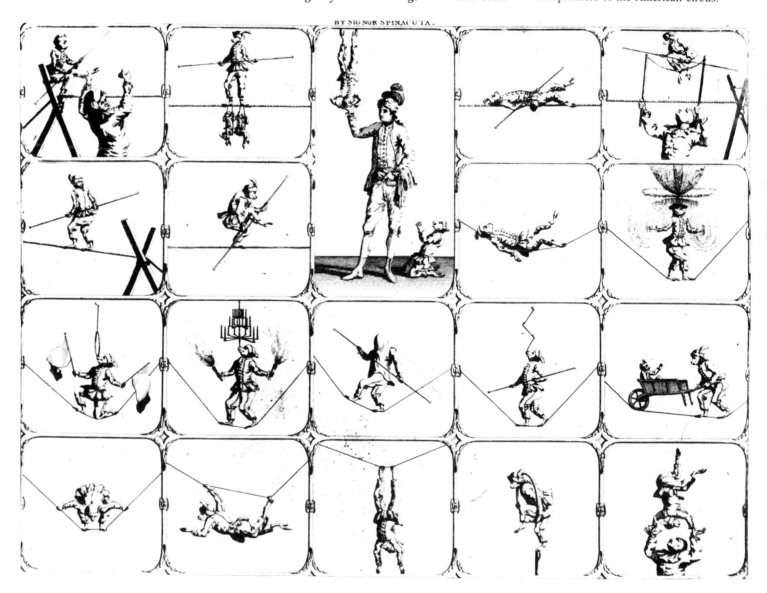

BY SIGNOR SPINACUTA.

IN PORTENTIS GLORIANT

NON PLUS ULTRA

Top An eighteenth-century French handbill, probably for 'Mahomet Achmed Vizaro Mussulmo', a fashionable rope-dancer.

Above A rope-walker at Bartholomew Fair.

Opposite A broadsheet illustrates the many popular entertainments, including circus acts, which could be seen at a London fair.

acquaintance with a fellow who carried me to a tavern, whither came the music of this booth, and by and by Jacob Hall himself, with whom I had a mind to speak, whether he ever had any mischief of falls in his time. He told me: ''Yes, many, but never to the breaking of a limb.'' He seems a mighty strong man. So giving them a bottle or two of wine, I away.'

Hall, besides dancing on the rope, was an acrobat, adept at flip-flaps and somersaulting over men holding aloft naked rapiers and through hoops. He was the first lover of Nell Gwynne, but that did not last long for Nell soon transferred her favours elsewhere.

Juggling and other feats were performed on the rope. At Bartholomew Fair, in 1701, Barnes danced on the rope with two children at his feet and wearing boots and spurs. In 1741 Hussey's booth, pitched in George Yard, Whitechapel, had a tremendous attraction in the slack-rope walker, Mahomet Achmed Vizaro Mussulmo, a Turk said to have just arrived in London from Constantinople. Among other feats he played a violin while on the rope. There is an old print depicting him in various attitudes: with his head on the rope, sitting on a board balanced on the rope, balancing an axe on his nose, holding flaming torches in his hands, and pushing with his knees along the rope a wheelbarrow with a man sitting inside. A century later and one would have suspected the hand of Barnum in this incredible advertisement. At the end of the eighteenth century the Count d'Artois had lessons in rope-dancing of Forioso and in 1805, holding a pole and dancing, he walked across a rope stretched from bank to bank of the Seine.

The fact that most of these artists came from the Mediterranean suggests, at least to us, that the art had been fairly continuous from the Circus Maximus onwards. Even if it was a pale shadow of its former self, at least the spirit of these circus acts was less cruel than the old.

THE FAIR.

Off to the Fair.

Harry Galloping to it

Receiving a Fairing.

Going to Spend it.

Fine Salmon !

A Blow Up !

Punch & his Wife.

Conjuring.

Players.

Wonderful Doings.

A Merry Dance.

Only Twopence !

Tyger.

Master & Servant.

Bear & Monkey.

Funny Jaques.

Odd Fellows.

Masquerade.

Get Home !

The Flogging.

Peep at London.

Horsemanship.

The Mountebank.

Printed and sold by J. and C. EVANS, 42, Long-Lane, West Smithfield, London.

Entertainment at the French court in the eighteenth century: some performers play musical instruments whilst balancing on a tight-rope.

Opposite Late eighteenth-century French watercolours showing a slack-rope dancer and an acrobat balancing on a candlestick.

Astley's Amphitheatre

It was the horse which was the last living creature to draw his racing chariot from the circus of the Ancient World; it was the horse, more than a thousand years later, which led the way into the Ring which Philip Astley enclosed on a piece of ground in Lambeth known as 'Ha'penny Hatch' and started to give exhibitions of riding there.

Stories of his early life and heroism in the army need not be utterly discounted but have the inescapable air of legend about them. Certainly he was born on 8 January 1742 at Newcastle-under-Lyme. We know nothing of his mother; all we know of his father, who was a cabinet-maker, was that he had a violent temper. Young Philip was early set to work on the bench of his father's workshop but he had no great liking for planing, shaping, sawing and hammering; in his blood was a passion for horses and already he knew as much about riding, harnessing and grooming as he did of cabinet-making. So, like many other famous men, he played truant while he was an apprentice, dashing out of the workshop and idling his time away in watching the arrival and departure of the stage-coaches. When he sneaked back there would be the menacing figure of his father, strap in hand. So it went on until the boy was seventeen when, in the middle of one of his fierce quarrels with his father, he snatched the strap from his hand, threw it on the floor and left the workshop for good.

He journeyed south via Coventry where many people were on the road to the November Horse Fair. Young Astley fell in with a farmer with the horses he was taking to market and had the good luck to ride one. The year was 1759, the fourth of the Seven Years War. The English were leagued along the Elbe with the armies of Frederick the Great against the French. The Battle of Minden, where the English had achieved a great triumph, a single line of infantry breaking through and routing three lines of enemy cavalry, was still stirring the minds of Englishmen at home. Every street corner in Coventry had a scarlet-coated recruiting sergeant with tales of the glories and rewards of military life. As Astley wandered through the streets he caught the stentorian tone of one shouting: 'Here's Colonel Eliott, aide-de-camp to His Majesty King George, come here to enlist you in his new regiment, the 15th Dragoons. Let powdered hair, drums and colours speak for themselves and if you have a mind to wet your whistles with His Majesty's double beer, follow me.' Young Astley's blood was fired. Here was his future beckoning plain, and with 'I'm your man!' he turned and followed the sergeant.

It is at this point that the story grows more legendary. Young Philip, we are told, was at once set to breaking-in some new mounts. Having efficiently done this, he was made a corporal with the pay of 'rough rider, teacher and breaker'. In the grounds of Lord Pembroke's house at Wilton, where Astley had come for instruction in the new method

Opposite Nineteenth-century French posters showing the extraordinary skills attributed to human and animal performers.

Above Astley started his circus with displays of horsemanship. His first horse, Billy, a gift from the commander of his regiment, was intelligent enough to perform special tricks.

Below Astley's riding-school, situated near Westminster Bridge, was financed by the lucky find of a diamond ring.

Bottom The Royal Circus owned by Charles Hughes, Astley's rival.

of cavalry riding which Domenico Angelo was trying to persuade the Government to adopt, 'his agility and mastery over the horse so astonished the common people in the neighbourhood that they thought Corporal Astley was the devil in disguise'. They might have been surprised enough at seeing a man ride full speed standing upon his horse and then leap off and mount again without the horse slackening his pace, but they must have been astonished when his horse cantered round a circle, with Astley upon his back standing upon his head with his heels in the air.

Two years later, with his regiment, he embarked at Tilbury for Germany. When the troopships were moored off Hamburg and while Astley was supervising the landing of the horses, one, rearing with terror, over-balanced and fell into the water. A strong tide

running, the animal was swimming out to sea when Astley dived in after it, caught it by the bridle and swam with the horse back to the boat. The reward for this feat was a third stripe. It was not long before the regiment was in action at Emsdorf where again Astley distinguished himself. Surrounded by French infantrymen, his horse shot from under him and wounded himself, he cut his way to safety, still however grasping a captured enemy standard. At Warburg the Duke of Brunswick was unhorsed in the enemy lines. Astley, followed by four dragoons, charged to his rescue. There was a desperate skirmish, followed by heavy fire, as Astley with the Duke safely in charge galloped back to the English lines.

In 1760 the regiment was recalled to England. At a parade in Hyde Park Sergeant-

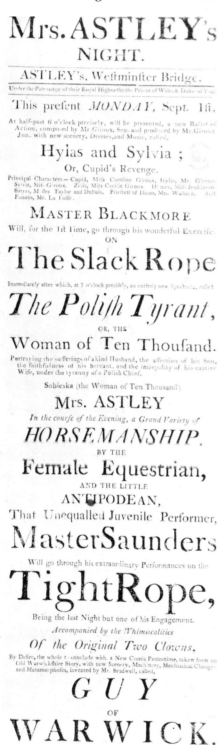

Far left Handbill for Astley's after its expansion to encompass a variety of acts, including the first clowns to appear in the ring.

Left Poster advertising Cooke's Royal Circus, the first to tour the country.

41

Several of the principal Nobility, now in Town, having solicited Mr. ASTLEY to exhibit the Whole of his Activity on One, Two, Three, and Four Horses, with all his other Amusements, on One Night; therefore gives Notice, that this and every Evening, till Monday next,

The grand general Display will be made in a brilliant Manner.

By PARTICULAR DESIRE,

The Whole of these amazing various Exhibitions, under the following Titles, viz.

HORSEMANSHIP, or ACTIVITY,

By Mr. and Mrs. ASTLEY, &c. &c. &c.

The BROAD-SWORD as in Real ACTION.

HEAVY BALLANCING, and Horsemanship BURLESQU'D.

With a COMIC RACE in Sacks, by Four Capital Performers in that Art.

ALSO,

Comus, Jonas, & Breslaw's Tricks, with Sleeve Buttons, Watches, Purses, Money, Letters, Cards, &c.

By the Little Learned MILITARY HORSE,

(With a short instructive Lecture on each by Mr. ASTLEY.) Also

The Magical Tables: Or, the Little Horse turn'd Conjurer.

In Four GRAND CHANGES.

With Variety of other Exhibitions, to make the General Nights complete.

To begin at a Quarter before Six o'Clock precisely———Admittance One Shilling each, though not the Tenth Part of the Value of such an extraordinary Performance.

*** Mr. ASTLEY has been at a very great Expence in making Preparations for the General Nights, in Order to accommodate the Nobility in an elegant manner, therefore flatters himself, the Variety and Drollness of the several Exhibitions cannot fail of giving the greatest Satisfaction to every Beholder, as there never was a Performance of its Kind at One Place in Europe.

N. B. Mr. Astley thought only to make one General Night, but as the Weather might prove uncertain, and the Night fixed on might not suit every one, and willing to oblige the Nobility, Gentry and others, with such an extraordinary Sight, continues it till Monday next, being positively the last Night.

†§† It is humbly requested the Nobility will be in good Time, in order to see the whole general Display.

Servants to keep Places to be at the Door precisely at Four o'Clock, when Mr. Astley will be very punctual in securing such Places as they shall request.

Major Astley was presented to the aged George II in his tent and laid the Emsdorf standard at his feet. With this culmination of his military career Astley now resolved to have done with the Army, for already his ambition was centred on establishing a riding-school for the nobility. At Derby, where he was billeted, he was told that the new landlord of an imposing inn had gained the purchase money by trick-riding on horseback in a field and then going round with a hat. Astley determined immediately that he would acquire the purchase money for his riding-school in exactly the same way. He went to Sir William Erskine, then in command of the regiment, and asked for his discharge. Not only was this granted 'in consideration of his general proper demeanour', as the certificate of service stated, but Sir William also presented him with a white charger. It was on this that Astley rode when he again turned his way south. In London he met and married the 'lovely Mrs Smith', a horsewoman. At Smithfield he purchased a little pony, as a wedding present for her. 'This here hanimal' he said to Mrs Smith 'has eyes bright, lively, resolute and himpudent that will look at an hobject with a kind of disdain.' For the same sum he acquired another horse and yet another; but the first, Billy, was always his favourite, for Billy could perform all the tricks as well as others that Zucker's Learned Little Horse did at the Belvedere Tea Gardens, Pentonville.

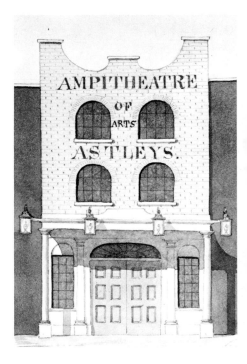

He seems to have had little respect for the rights of property, for the field he appropriated at Ha'penny Hatch was simply fenced off with rope and stakes; an area now covered by the platforms of Waterloo Station. In the late afternoons of those days Astley, dressed in all the splendour of his military uniform and astride his white charger, took up a position on the south side of Westminster Bridge, distributing handbills and pointing with his sword to the pathway which meandered over the fields to Ha'penny Hatch. This gave rise to yet another tall story, that George III, an excellent horseman, while riding across the bridge one afternoon had lost control of a very spirited mount. Astley galloped to his rescue and gave the king a demonstration of his skill in handling horses. But Decastro in his charming memoirs gives a far different version. Decastro states that the king, accompanied by the Duke of York, was riding over the bridge when he observed Astley at his daily post flourishing his sword and shouting to the passers-by. 'Who is that, Frederick?' the king enquired of the Duke of York. 'Mr Astley, sir. One of our good friends, a veteran, one that fought in the German war.' Hearing this, the king turned and gave Astley a courteous salutation. For long after Astley would relate to all he met: 'My Sovereign did me the honour to bow to me: what d'you think of that now?'

For a time at Ha'penny Hatch Astley contented himself with a collection at the end of each performance, but later, having built a rough shelter for some of his audience, his handbills announced: 'Activity on horseback of Mr Astley, Sergeant-Major in His Majesty's Royal Regiment of Light Dragoons. Nearly twenty different attitudes will be performed on one, two and three horses every evening during the summer at his riding-school. Doors to be open at four and he will mount at five. Seats, one shilling; standing-places, sixpence.' Five years later these prices had been doubled.

In the centre of the ground was a pigeon-house and during performances a boy sat in this beating a drum to whip up some excitement; this was Astley's first band and the first circus band. Soon the receipts were as much as forty guineas a day. In the midst of this success Mrs Astley temporarily retired from the ring and gave birth to a son, called John.

Ha'penny Hatch was soon to prove inadequate for Philip's purposes, so he began to look about for a more adequate and favourable site. On the south side of Westminster Bridge he discovered a corner site owned by an old man, who had a preserve of pheasants there; but the preserve brought him no profit and he was in dire need of £200. In 1769 a mortgage was completed between him and Astley, and Astley became the owner of the property. And at this point he benefited from two extremely lucky incidents. Crossing Westminster Bridge he picked up a diamond ring valued at seventy guineas, and as this was never advertised for or claimed Astley sold it and on the proceeds was able to commence his new building. Then a month or so later the mortgagor went abroad and was not heard of again. He left behind a quantity of timber which was invaluable to Astley who did not hesitate to use it. The new establishment was opened in 1770. A penthouse partly covered the seats around 'the drive', as the ring was then called, and this gave cover to the higher-priced places. Astley now advertised performances 'every evening, wet or dry'. Steps ascended from the road to the entrance, where a green curtain covered the door behind which Mrs Astley stood to take the

Opposite An eighteenth-century handbill for Astley's, showing how Mrs Astley cooperated in the acts.

Above Frontage of the Amphitheatre of Arts, built on the Westminster site after the original circus was destroyed by fire in 1794.

Below A poster advertising Astley's Circus in 1843, continuing to use his name long after his death.

Right A delightful equestrienne at Astley's such as Dickens might well have seen.

money. The exterior walls of the building were whitewashed and covered with pictorial posters of the various acts, while along the top of the building were painted cut-out figures of horses and riders in a number of attitudes. One of the first bills announced that: 'Mr Astley exhibits, at full speed, the different cuts and guards made use of by Eliott's [men] the Prussian and the Hessian Hussars. Also the manner of Eliott's [men] charging the French troops in Germany, in the year 1761, when it was said that the regiment were all tailors.'

From the first Astley had sensed that his performances were lacking in variety. By energetic teaching he had created no other performers beside himself, his wife, his pony Billy and his white charger. Now, at the opening performance at his new establishment, he introduced 'Chinese Shadows', 'Tumbling', 'Slack-rope Vaulting in full swing, in different attitudes', 'Egyptian Pyramids' and the first clown to enter a ring, a man named Burt. Astley had thus established the first modern circus and the great circus proprietors of the last century-and-a-half are no more than his successors.

To advertise his performances he now paraded the West End streets, leading the procession in his inevitable military uniform and riding his 'richly caparisoned' white charger. Behind him strutted two trumpeters and two equestrians in their stage costume, while at the rear came a coach in which sat the 'learned pony' and a clown who distributed handbills.

The centre of his riding-school was open to the air, an inconvenience when the weather was bad. This Astley circumvented in characteristic fashion. As early as 1772 he had purchased at an absurdly low price timber which had been used for scaffolding at the funeral of Augusta, Princess Dowager of Wales, and in 1780 he added to this store through one of those lucky incidents of which he was quick to take advantage. There had been an election and following the result the mob began demolishing the hustings to make bonfires, as was usual on such occasions. Astley, mingling with the rabble, shouted in his stentorian voice that he would give beer for the timber if it was carried to his establishment. 'Beer' he roared 'is better than bonfires!' The crowd thought so too. He obtained enough wood not only to cover his riding-school but also to remodel it, adding a stage, two tiers of boxes, a pit and a gallery. The interior of the dome-shaped roof was painted to represent tree branches and leaves and it was this decoration which caused Astley to call the building 'The Royal Grove'. Now when day faded to evening candles were lit and the performances continued with this illumination.

Astley's young son made his first appearance in the ring, riding on one and two horses. On the bills his age was given as five, although actually he was ten. While his

horse was at full gallop Master Astley danced, vaulted and played the violin.

Now that he was a success in the world Astley looked for a reconciliation with his old father. As a result Edward Astley and Philip's sister, of whom he was very fond, came to join him in London where she quickly found someone to marry. Philip and his father got on no better than in the old days. Their quarrels grew in intensity until in 1782 the old man swore before the Lord Mayor that his son frequently assaulted him, had turned him out of doors and 'used him with such unbecoming abuse and scurrilous language that

An engraving of the ring at the Royal Circus, St George's Fields, showing an equestrian act in progress.

the deponent cannot, without impropriety, state the same in a public paper'. What had led to a final showdown between father and son was the mortification Philip felt that his father 'had thought proper to engage as a doorkeeper to a place of public amusement'. Old Astley, now being destitute, had been engaged 'through charity' by Charles Hughes, Philip's bitterest enemy, the proprietor of the competing Royal Circus, to distribute handbills on Blackfriars Bridge at a wage of half a guinea a week. This was a humiliating affront to Philip and he and Hughes entered into litigation with each other. Finally Philip's father became Hughes's ostler.

Beginning in 1772, Astley regularly every year took his troupe to Paris and performed there. These visits were interrupted by the war of 1778-83. In 1783 Horace Walpole wrote to a friend complaining that he could find nothing to do in London 'and so went to Astley's, which indeed was much beyond my expectations . . . But I shall not even have Astley now; Her Majesty the Queen of France has sent for the whole of the *dramatis personae* to Paris.' It was true. Astley was again in Paris. At Versailles young John danced a minuet on three horses. Marie-Antoinette, delighted with 'his manly agility, symmetry of figure, elegance of attitude and gentlemanly deportment' gave him a gold medal magnificently set with diamonds and called him 'The English Rose', the French Rose being Vestris, whose dancing had charmed and captivated Parisians.

Astley's *ménage* performed in the open air in the *faubourg du Temple*. Every day the place was thronged while the theatres, the opera and the ballet houses had empty benches. Royal patronage was promised for forthcoming visits, and on the strength of this and his success Astley chose a site for an *Amphithéâtre Anglais*. This became an imposing building with roof, stage and musicians' gallery, while twelve hundred jets of flame shot from thirty candelabra to give superb illumination. But in 1787 Astley was warned by the Prefect of Police that his tumbling acts were an infringement of the law which enacted that there be no duplication of entertainments in the Parisian theatres. Astley grinned. His carpenters made a large wooden platform. This, in the ring, was supported by horses and on it his acrobats performed. The performance was now equestrian and therefore legal! The French Revolution and the fall of the Bastille again stopped his appearances in Paris.

In 1792 war broke out between England and France. Astley assisted in the embarkation of the cavalry horses at Deptford and Gravesend, then rejoined his old

Undaunted by the burning down of the Amphitheatre of the Arts, Astley constructed a fine new building known as the Royal Amphitheatre of the Arts.

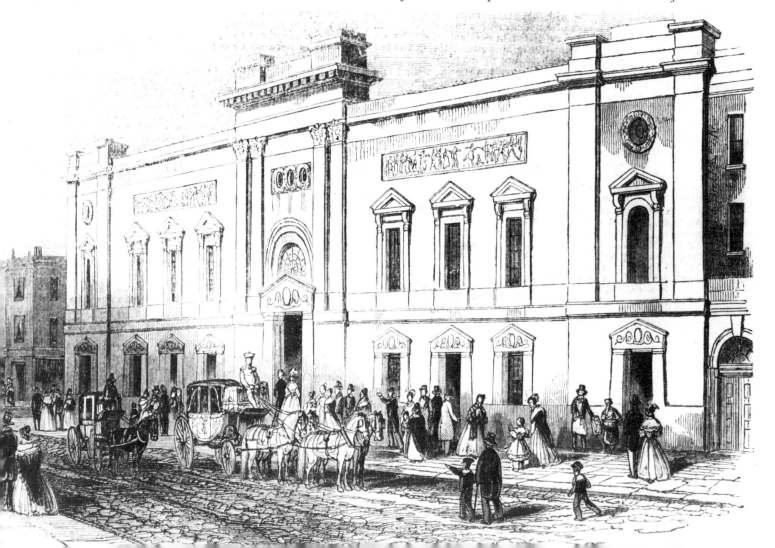

regiment, the 15th Light Dragoons, as a volunteer. He was soon characteristically in the limelight, for at Ribecourt his cunning enabled him to recover a gun captured by the French. The Duke of York, delighted with this exploit, rewarded him with the four horses which had constituted the gun-carriage team. Astley put them up to auction and spent the purchase money on wine for the troops. He had already presented the men of the 15th with needles, thread, buttons, bristles, twine and leather to mend their clothes and shoes. Each man had also received a flannel waistcoat which Astley had set his female employees at The Royal Grove to make. Sewn in the corner of each garment was what Astley called 'a friend in need', a new shilling. He also saw to it that his patriotic

generosity was widely paragraphed in the newspapers, so that the subsequent increase in the nightly receipts at The Royal Grove more than paid for the cost of the flannel and 'the friend in need'.

In 1794 The Royal Grove together with nineteen adjoining houses was completely destroyed by fire. Astley came post-haste from the Continent. Not in the least daunted by the devastation, he immediately gave orders that rebuilding should commence on a grandiose scale. The new house was opened in the following year and called The Amphitheatre of Arts.

When the Peace of Amiens was signed in 1802, Astley returned to Paris. Finding his circus in the *faubourg du Temple* had been used as a barracks by the Revolutionary Government, he petitioned Bonaparte for compensation. Much to his own amazement as well as everybody else's, compensation was granted. Hardly had he pocketed the money when hostilities were renewed, and Englishmen then in France were confined as prisoners of war; so that Astley had to escape to the frontier disguised as a wounded French officer.

In London he was greeted with tragic news. His wife was dead, his theatre a smoking

Astley's had begun life as a riding-school and always retained its equestrian tradition. Here, a trick rider, Jean Polaski, astonishes the audience with his daring feat.

ruin. For a second time it had been utterly destroyed by fire. The charred remains of his mother-in-law, Mrs Woodham, had been found in the debris. But Astley's courage was indomitable. On the following Easter Monday another theatre was opened on the same site: Astley's Royal Amphitheatre of the Arts.

Astley's music at his riding-school on Ha'penny Hatch had been the beating of a drum. Subsequently he added a fife, the players standing on a small platform in the centre of the ring. It was not until he opened The Royal Grove that he had the music of a band. In many respects, and despite his enterprise, Astley was extremely ignorant. There is the well-known story of his rebuking a bandsman because at a rehearsal he was not playing. The man explained that there was a rest. 'A rest!' thundered Astley. 'I don't pay you to rest, but to play!' Once hearing a manager complain of the conduct of his actors he remarked: 'Why don't you treat them as I do my horses? I never give them anything to eat until their performance is done.' He considered the most desirable quality in a band was loudness and although he invariably engaged skilled musicians he had a feeling that they were an unnecessary expense. 'Any fool,' he would say, 'can handle a fiddle, but it takes a man to manage a horse. Yet I have to pay a fellow who plays upon one fiddle as much salary as a man that rides upon three horses.'

Astley was a master at butchering the King's English. One authority quotes him as describing 'a crocodile wat stopped Halexander's harmy and when cut hopen had a man in harmour in its hintellects,' and in confidential mood declaring he would be a ruined man for 'these here horses eat most vociferously.' When in France he uttered his most celebrated Malapropism when he whispered to his son during the Versailles visit: 'That there King can't be the father of the Dolphin. Why, he's *Omnipotent!*'

But although he was uneducated – and there is little evidence that he ever received more than the most elementary of schooling – Astley was endowed with a strong mind and an acute understanding. He was noted for his eccentric habits and peculiarities of

The splendid interior of Astley's Amphitheatre depicted by Rowlandson. It housed both a stage and a ring so that Victorian audiences could enjoy circus performances as well as productions of melodramatic plays.

An equestrian act at Franconi's Olympic Circus in Paris, one of the most ambitious circus buildings of all time.

behaviour. One of his idiosyncrasies was revealed after his second fire. A man came to dun him for immediate payment of a large bill. Astley produced the money from a secret store of guineas which he had hoarded for years. He had, in fact, a difficult nature, made few friends and quickly lost the few he made. Yet he was always respected. What affections he had seemed to be centred on his wife and sister. But even these had their vicissitudes. Among his papers after his death were found scraps of doggerel verse in which were allusions to his wife and son, invariably unkind.

As a breaker and trainer of horses he was unequalled in his time; his treatise on horse training can still be read with interest and advantage. He schooled each horse by itself and in a place where there was no noise or other disturbing factor to distract its attention. When the horse had perfected certain lessons it was placed with other horses in a more advanced stage of schooling. When they performed well Astley rewarded them with slices of apple or carrot. He was the first in modern times to teach horses to dance, his animals going through the figures and apparently stepping in time to the music. His favourite horse, Billy, used to lift a kettle from the fire and arrange the tea-things for company. He was a playful animal and romped with Astley and the grooms as a kitten would.

In 1813, when he was seventy-two, he went to Paris hoping to be cured of a disorder and there he died on 20 October 1814 in his old home in the *rue du Temple*. He was buried in Père Lachaise cemetery. Seven years later his son John, worn out although still but middle-aged, also went to Paris, suffering from a complaint of the liver. And there, too, within a day of that on which his father died, he died on 19 October 1821 in the same house and in the same bed as his father, later joining him in the same cemetery. His widow had a gravestone erected over his remains on which was inscribed 'The Once Rose of Paris'.

Some twenty years after Philip Astley's death, Charles Dickens knew Astley's well and wrote of it in *The Old Curiosity Shop*. His description is valuable and gives us an idea of just what Astley's had become, that is, a stage on which melodramas were acted combined with a circus ring in which circus acts were performed.

Dickens describes Kit's visit to Astley's with his mother, Barbara, Barbara's mother and little Jacob. The description is sentimental but vivid, like so many of Dickens's descriptions:

Dear, dear, what a place it looked, that Astley's; with all the paint, gilding, and looking-glass; the vague smell of horses suggestive of coming wonders; the curtain that hid such gorgeous mysteries; the clean white sawdust down in the circus; the company coming in and taking their places; the fiddlers looking carelessly up at them while they tuned their instruments, as if they didn't want the play to begin, and knew it all beforehand! What a glow was that, which burst upon them all, when that long, clear, brilliant row of lights came slowly up; and what the feverish excitement when the little bell rang and the music began in good earnest, with strong parts for the drums, and sweet effects for the triangles! Well might Barbara's mother say to Kit's mother that the gallery was the place to see from, and wonder it wasn't much dearer than the boxes: well might Barbara feel doubtful whether to laugh or cry, in her flutter of delight.

Then the play itself! the horses which little Jacob believed from the first to be alive, and the ladies and gentlemen of whose reality he could be by no means persuaded, having never seen or heard anything at all like them – the firing, which made Barbara wink – the forlorn lady, who made her cry – the tyrant, who made her tremble – the man who sang the song with the lady's-maid and danced the chorus, who made her laugh – the pony who reared up on his hind legs when he saw the murderer, and wouldn't hear of walking on all-fours again until he was taken into custody – the clown who ventured on such familiarities with the military man in boots – the lady who jumped over the nine-and-twenty ribbons and came down safe upon the horse's back – everything was delightful, splendid, and surprising! Little Jacob applauded till his hands were sore; Kit cried 'an-kor' at the end of everything, the three-act piece included; and Barbara's mother beat her umbrella on the floor, in her ecstasies, until it was nearly worn down to the gingham.

An elephant performing a trick at Astley's at the end of the last century.

Barnum and Ballyhoo

While Astley was still the unchallenged founder of the circus in Europe several of his assistants and competitors became enterprising creators and performers in the United States, and they were so successful that before the middle of the nineteenth century American showmen were invited over to dazzle English and French audiences. The enterprises and partnerships of these early pioneers, their foundations and failure are almost impossible to follow in detail down to the rise of the Ringling Brothers, who in 1907 purchased the Barnum and Bailey 'Greatest Show on Earth' and combined it with their own, to form the colossus which exists today.

That is not to say that a number of picturesque characters were lacking from the early American circus. A rival of Astley's, Charles Hughes, had trained a brilliant young rider named John Bill Ricketts to be one of the best trick equestrians on Astley's bill, and Ricketts had emigrated to the United States, or perhaps remained after the British forces went home after the Revolution. He started a riding-school at the corner of Twelfth and Market Streets in Philadelphia, exactly as Astley had started at Ha'penny Hatch in London. The story goes that General George Washington was impressed when Ricketts leapt over a number of horses – *ten* it is claimed – with a boy on his shoulder 'in the attitude of Mercury' and danced a hornpipe on the saddle while his horse galloped round the ring. If there is any truth in this the circus could scarcely have found a better and more influential patron than the great man, and one may be sure that Ricketts knew how to take advantage of this. Certainly in 1795 he was performing at the 'Greenwich Theatre near the Battery' in New York. Here he showed his riding and acrobatic acts, supported by Signor Reano on the slack-wire and Mr William Sully, a vocalist 'late of Sadler's Wells, London', singing 'Four and Twenty Periwigs'. When John Bill Ricketts returned for a season to Philadelphia it was, according to one authority, 'in a circular building nearly a hundred feet in diameter, especially erected for circus purposes, at the corner of Sixth and Chestnut Streets. Signor Spinacuta was actively with him. So was Mrs Spinacuta, who rode two horses at full gallop, the Polander Dwarf, who leaped through a hoop of fire, and a trained horse, Cornplanter, which leaped over another horse fifty-six inches in height.'

But Ricketts was an Englishman and not surprisingly he soon had American-born rivals. Rufus Welch was probably the first of these, who in 1818 managed a wagon show and before long was directing more ambitious enterprises. In November 1826 the Mount Pitt Circus opened on Broome Street, New York, in a building seating 3,500 persons, said at that time to be the largest place of amusement in America. Other early circuses were those of 'Old' John Robinson, Dick Sands and Van Amburgh, the two last-named making European tours in the forties.

Ricketts' Circus.

THIS DAY, the 15th of May, At the Circus in Market, the Corner of Twelfth streets. The Doors will be Opened at 4, and the Performance begin at half past Five o'clock, precisely

Will be Performed—A Great Variety of Equestrian Exercises,

By Mr. & Master *Ricketts*, Master *Strobach*, and Mr. *M'Donald*, who is just arrived from Europe.

In the Course of the Entertainment, Mr. Ricketts will introduce several *New Feats*, particularly he will Ride with his Knees on the Saddle, the Horse in full speed; and from this Position *Leap over a Ribband* extended 12 feet high.

Mr. *Ricketts*, on a single Horse, will throw up 4 Oranges, playing with them in the Air, the Horse in full speed.

Mr. *M'Donald* will Perform several COMIC FEATS (Being his First Appearance in America).

Seignior *Spiracuta* will exhibit many Surprizing Feats on the Tight Rope.

The whole to conclude with Mr. Ricketts and his Pupil in the Attitudes of two Flying Mercuries; the Boy pois'd on one Foot on Mr Ricketts' Shoulder, whilst Mr. Ricketts stands in the same Manner with one Foot on the Saddle, the Horse being in full speed.

✱ Those Ladies and Gentlemen who wish to embrace the present Opportunity of seeing the Exercises of the Circus, are respectfully informed, that Mr. *Ricketts* intends closing it for the Season within three Weeks from the present Time, as he is about to take a Tour to some other Parts of the Continet

Tickets sold at Mr Bradford's Book Store, Front street, and at the Circus.

Box 7/6 – Pit 3/9.

Advertisement for Ricketts' circus. Ricketts was an ex-Astley performer who emigrated to America to found his own show.

NO DRAFTIN' IN BALDINSVILLE.

THE FIRST OF A SERIES OF ORIGINAL LETTERS ON THE WAR, WRITTEN EXPRESSLY FOR VANITY FAIR, BY ARTEMUS WARD, WILL APPEAR IN OUR NEXT NUMBER.

THEY WILL BE CONTINUED WEEKLY.

VOL. 6.   NO. 142.

Saturday,
SEPT. 13,
1862.

PRICE TWO DOLLARS PER ANNUM—SINGLE COPIES SIX CENTS.

PUBLISHED EVERY SATURDAY, AT 113 NASSAU STREET, N.Y.

PHINEAS TAYLOR BARNUM:

BLOWING, WITH ALL HIS MIGHT, FOR HIS "HAPPY FAMILY," THE CONFIDING PUBLIC.

A rather later but more enterprising impresario was Adam Forepaugh, a Philadelphia butcher, who not only ran successful circuses but invented that corral of smirking young women which came to be called 'The Beauty Contest'. In 1880 he offered a prize for America's most beautiful woman which resulted in the selection of a girl named Louise Montague who afterwards rode in his circus parade as 'The $10,000 Beauty'.

Another innovator was Lewis B. Lent in whose historic New York Theatre the circus played during the winter months in 14th Street opposite the old Academy of Music, but exhibited 'Brown and Lent's' up and down the Mississippi and Ohio rivers in the 1860s and 70s, at the same time being the first circus to travel by rail. Contemporary portraits show Lent as a prolifically hirsute man wearing starched linen under his somewhat clerical clothes. Like others of the time he played musical chairs with partnerships, passing from Welch, with whom he took his menagerie and circus to Spain, France, Italy and Brazil, and later teaming with Dick Sands when that smart showman was also in partnership with John J. Nathan who introduced a four-horse carrying act and postured on horseback to crowded audiences.

Others who figured in the early American circus in various capacities, performers or owner-showmen, are numerous but few biographical details of them are recorded. Seth B. Howes, who had once accompanied his elder brother Nate on an elephant tour into Maine, became the founder and for years the owner-manager of 'Howes' Great London Circus', and it is interesting to note that the title was a profitable one in America, just as Cody's 'Wild West Show' was to London audiences. In 1857, as a partner to Joe Cushing, the energetic Howes took his show to England, featuring seventy cream-coloured horses; visited Queen Victoria at the Alhambra in London; and was rewarded by a cheque from the Royal Secretary for five hundred pounds.

Then there was Aaron Turner, a shoemaker of English descent, who taught his sons Napoleon B. and Timothy V. to make and build up a canvas enclosure, and with one or two others, and considerable courage, set out on a tenting season. They seem to have resisted the current temptation to form partnerships but remained an independent and ultimately successful show. Earl Chapin May describes their progress:

Opposite The front cover of *Vanity Fair* of September 1862 showed Phineas Taylor Barnum, the famous showman, blowing his own trumpet. This was before he took an interest in the circus proper.

Above left Dan Rice, a jack-of-all-trades, who made his fortune as a clown, but died a penniless alcoholic.

Above centre Miss Louise Montagu, who won a beauty contest in 1880 and rode in Forepaugh's circus as 'The $10,000 Beauty'.

Above right Lewis B. Lent, an early impresario whose circus was the first to travel by rail.

Mr Turner enlarged his circus. He presently went on tour with a round, center-poled canvas measuring ninety feet from sidewall to sidewall. In addition to several lengths of circus seats he lined his baggage wagons against his sidewall. Patrons who could not secure luxurious accommodations on hard, blue planks, could compose themselves on empty wagons.

Aaron's sons, Napoleon B. and Timothy V., increased their performing repertoire – in addition to tumbling, rope-walking and contortion, did some fancy riding and vaulting. Their sister became equally versatile. After the one-ring performance was 'all out and ovah' an 'Ethiopian entertainment' was offered, for negro minstrels had its start in our early circuses.

Yet, in spite of its radical expansion, a spirit of economy ruled old Turner's show. When Napoleon B. became a directing head as well as an artist, he was inclined to invest his circus surplus in a new hotel at Danbury, Conn. After he had used his red and gold bandwagon until it rotted, he insisted upon parading his six musicians in a baggage wagon. George F. Bailey, the general manager, established a precedent for circuses when he drove this box wagon onto the White House grounds at Washington and serenaded Andrew Jackson, President of the United States and 'Hero of New Orleans'. The substitute bandwagon met the approval of Old Hickory.

When Aaron *did* eventually succumb to the fashion for forming partnerships he chose wisely, for the company he formed was with Phineas T. Barnum, later the proprietor of 'The Greatest Show on Earth'. But they did not remain long together and, as we shall see, Barnum went on to more extravagant enterprises.

Another versatile trouper was Dan Rice, who entered the ring as a clown but fulfilled many other functions in his long and varied life. He is said to have graduated from Strong Man and part owner of a 'talking pig' which he introduced as 'Lord Byron'. He had been taught to ride by his stepfather and raced for some seasons before increased weight sent him to team up with a card-sharper working the river boats; he also wrote and performed a music-hall song called 'Hard Times'. But after some shady association with Joseph Smith, the founder of Mormonism, he reached his main objective as a clown in a circus owned by another remarkable character, Dr Gilbert R. Spaulding. From this occupation he was lured by Seth B. Howes, who made him the most advertised member of Mabie Brothers until Rufus Welch seized him as a most promising young clown. He became known as 'a Shakespearean actor and equestrian' who exchanged repartee with the audience and has been called the precursor of Will Rogers. Earl Chapin May continues:

> You get a slight idea of the man's strength and versatility when you read in the record that he won a dancing contest while with Old John Robinson's Circus; sang Old-Log-Cabin songs when Benjamin Harrison was running for President; when first engaged by Dr Spaulding, not only sang comic songs, did a special clown act, played a negro part in the inevitable 'Ethiopian entertainment', caught genuine cannon balls on the back of his neck and performed other feats of super-strength and agility, but also stood ready to lick any three men who would tackle him after the big show was all out and over. For this catholicity of endeavour he received $15.00 per week and 'keep'. From the earliest days of American circuses performers have signed contracts with owners or managers in which a clause requires that 'said performer shall make himself generally useful'. Dan Rice, though a star, was not above general usefulness. And he never lost a fistic battle.

The story after this is what must be expected. He came to own a successful circus but dissipated his capital by wilful generosity and alcoholism, and died penniless. But in circus annals he lives as King of American Clowns, and his latter-day fate was no harsher than those which rewarded other artists like William Collins Foster and Edgar Allen Poe in that philistine epoch in the New World.

Of others little more than the name on old playbills and a legend or two survives. Joe Pentland, a clown, would sit among the audience appearing to be a drunken sailor until the riding act, when he would challenge the equestrienne to let him ride, and fall off again and again. The audience loved it and loved the dénouement when Pentland pulled off his sailor's uniform to reveal spangles and ride brilliantly round the ring. Other impresarios before Barnum and Bailey and the Ringlings were John J. June, Lewis B. Titus, Caleb Sutton Angevine, Jeremiah Crane and Orton and Older. There were also Isaac Quick and a partner named Mead who shipped their circus by schooner from New York City to Richmond, Virginia, in 1826, taking in their company young Levi J. North, afterwards a well known and accomplished equestrian said to be the first in modern

Opposite top Scéne de Cirque by C. Lagar, 1922. Petit Palais, Geneva.

Opposite bottom Chevaux de Cirque by Cosson. Petit Palais, Geneva.

times to turn a somersault on a running horse. William Bill Lewis was reputed to have driven twenty horses in one hitch, holding ten long lines in each hand.

But here we must interpose the life-story of a man who outshone all showmen of the modern circus, British, American or European—the phenomenal Phineas T. Barnum, 'the Prince of Humbugs' as he was flatteringly called, a cognomen in which he took pleasure. He came late in life to the sawdust ring but his score of years as 'The Great Barnum' revolutionized the modern circus.

He was born in the small township of Bethel, Connecticut, on 5 July 1810, seven years after Ricketts had toured with the first circus in America. Phineas was the eldest of five children. His father was farmer, tailor, tavern-keeper, livery-stable proprietor and country-store merchant, but despite this versatility not a very successful businessman. Phineas was put to school when he was six and afterwards recalled that his first three teachers, a Mr Camp, a Mr Zerah Judson and a Mr Curtiss, all 'used the ferule prodigiously'. His schooling did not amount to much; he excelled at arithmetic but at nothing else. He was often kept away to help his father on the farm and this gave him an aversion to any kind of manual labour, so that he became known as the laziest boy in the town. But what he called his 'organ of acquisitiveness' was soon apparent. While still a small boy he earned money by selling cherry-rum to the soldiers and by the time he was twelve he had bought a sheep and a calf and saved a not inconsiderable sum from which his father made him buy his own clothes. Realising that Phineas would never be of the slightest use on a farm, his father now purchased a store and installed Phineas there as clerk. Goods in small towns were bartered then and Phineas was in his element when it came to driving hard bargains with the old countrywomen who, in payment for the purchases, tendered butter, eggs, beeswax and rags.

When the weather was bad there was no business and on those days Barnum would hobnob with 'from six to twenty social, jolly, storytelling, joke-playing wags and wits, regular originals'. They foregathered at the store or in the tavern, spinning yarns and playing practical jokes on one another, sharpening their wits with Santa Cruz rum or old Holland gin. It was on these occasions that Phineas was initiated and schooled in the Connecticut Yankee tradition of trying to get the better of the other fellow, honestly or dishonestly. Many years later, in his book *The Humbugs of the World,* Barnum symbolized this period of his education with this story: 'A grocer who also served as a deacon called downstairs one morning before breakfast to his clerk: "John, have you watered the rum?" "Yes, sir." "And sanded the sugar?" "Yes, sir." "And dusted the pepper?" "Yes, sir." "And chicoried the coffee?" "Yes, sir." "Then come up to prayers."' Thus religion and sharp practice were reconciled. Barnum was reared in the fear of hell. When he was thirteen he would come home from the Methodist meeting and pray to God to take him out of existence if He would only save him, for, he said afterwards, he couldn't see much chance for himself otherwise, the way redemption was put at the prayer-meetings. He always regarded himself as a deeply religious man, but with the reservation that God looks after him who looks after himself.

Sunday after Sunday the Bethel Minister denounced the sin of gambling, but was never averse to organising a lottery in aid of his funds. Lotteries were then legal and a profitable source of income to Phineas when he was a boy of twelve or thirteen. He was a lottery manager and salesman, selling tickets to the workpeople employed in the local hat and comb factories.

When Phineas was fifteen his father died suddenly and was found to have been insolvent, for he had spent the savings which Phineas had entrusted to his care. In an effort to keep herself and her children Mrs Barnum struggled on with the cares of the tavern, while Phineas became the clerk in a village store a mile away. Here he ingratiated himself with the proprietor by successfully organising a lottery which shifted an old stock of tinware and green-glass bottles. And here he fell in love. Her name was Charity Hallett and she had come on Saturday afternoon to the village to buy a hat from the only milliner within a radius of miles – Aunt 'Rushia'. A tremendous storm burst and Phineas was told that Charity was afraid to return alone to Bethel while it was raging. As they drove along, 'the fair, rosy-cheeked, buxom girl, with beautiful white teeth' (as Barnum was later to write of her) told him she was a tailoress. That night 'her face haunted him', he could not sleep and when he saw her at morning service she was even more beautiful than he had imagined. But they were able to meet only once a week at Sunday chapel.

He said his life at the store was one of 'dog eat dog'. 'The customers cheated us . . . we cheated the customers. Each party expected to be cheated if it was possible.' When he

Opposite The French Blondin, suitably attired as a matelot, walks on knives across an imaginary chasm in this poster.

was seventeen he went to Brooklyn and opened a porterhouse there, almost immediately selling it at a profit and going to New York to become a bar-tender at another porterhouse. He made excursions to the theatre and became, so he said, 'a close critic'. Changing from job to job, in 1828 he was back again at Bethel as a partner with his grandfather in a new venture, a fruit and confectionery store which also sold ale and oysters. Again he dabbled in lottery tickets and met his Charity every Sunday. One day a stranger dropped in at the store and set Phineas's imagination whirling with his exciting stories. The stranger was Hackariah Bailey (no relation to James A. Bailey) and the first showman of the many whom Phineas would meet. Bailey had been the first to exhibit an elephant in America, and this with other entertainment enterprises had gained him a fortune.

When he was nineteen Phineas married his Charity. They went to New York for the wedding, for it was a secret from his mother, who knew his heart but did not greatly approve of his choice of a tailoress, though other Bethel citizens thought Charity too good for Phineas. Mrs Barnum's resentment lasted a month, after which Phineas and Charity were forgiven and asked to Sunday dinner.

Two years after this a wave of religious fanaticism swept the State. Revival meetings were held everywhere and the countryside was in a state of frenzy. It gave a peculiar power to the Ministers, who urged that only those openly professing faith in God should hold public office. This was too much for Barnum and he wrote long letters of protest to the local newspaper, letters which came back with the editor's regrets that he had not the space to publish them. Barnum declared that he dared not. Was it the hurt vanity of not seeing his name in print which then prompted him to buy press and types and begin the publication of his own newspaper, which he grandiloquently called *The Herald of Freedom*? From the first few numbers he was in trouble. A butcher, whom he accused of being a spy in 'the Democratic Party Caucus', sued him for libel and was awarded several hundred dollars as damages. Undaunted, Barnum next attacked a deacon and charged him with 'taking usury of an orphan boy'. There was another libel action, this time Barnum was fined one hundred dollars and sentenced to sixty days in the common jail. Here, in a carpeted and wall-papered cell, he received visitors at all hours of the day and continued to edit *The Herald of Freedom*. He became aware of the value of publicity, for his libels were the talk of the State and hundreds of new

Top Phineas T. Barnum, 'the Prince of Humbugs', aged 66.

Above Phineas T. Barnum with his family.

subscriptions poured in. His release was celebrated as a public event, and a specially composed ode was sung in the courtroom where he had been tried and sentenced, the Reverend Theophilus Fiske reading an eloquent oration on 'The Freedom of the Press'. 'A sumptuous repast' was served to a large gathering, followed by speeches and toasts which lasted the entire afternoon. Barnum was then escorted home in a coach, a marshal waving the National Standard leading the way, followed by a band of music and forty horsemen, with sixty carriages of citizens bringing up the rear. As the procession approached Bethel the band stridently burst into the strains of 'Home, Sweet Home'.

His prosperity did not long continue. *The Herald of Freedom* failed to keep its circulation and ceased to appear with the issue No 160. Biggest blow of all, a new law was passed prohibiting lotteries. So in the winter of 1835, Phineas, Charity and their daughter Caroline went to New York, to find they could not have arrived at a worse time. The city was devastated by a fire which gutted upwards of seven hundred buildings, and the effects were so widespread that banks suspended payment and famous mercantile concerns closed down.

Fortunately Phineas received unexpected and substantial payments of money he had written off as 'bad debts' and with these windfalls he opened a boarding-house. But his mind was elsewhere. He was musing on what he could exhibit which would attract the amusement-loving New York public. By chance he met a Mr Coley Bartram, who told him that he had just sold his interest in Joice Heth, a Negress aged 161 who had originally been owned by George Washington's father. Barnum immediately dashed off to Philadelphia where the Negress was being shown. He was delighted with what he saw. Joice Heth was blind; she had no teeth and her head was covered with a mat of thick and bushy grey hair, while the nails of her fingers and toes were four inches long. But she sang hymns and spoke of George Washington as 'dear little George' and of being present when he was born. She said she 'had raised him'. Her present owner was willing to sell for three thousand dollars, but Barnum had only five hundred. He bargained for one thousand and it was accepted. Back he rushed to New York, borrowed the additional five hundred dollars he needed and returned to Philadelphia to collect the Negress. With Joice Heth he entered show business. He hired an exhibition hall, frantically distributed handbills and interviewed editors. He well knew the value of newspaper paragraphs and he got all he wanted.

In New York the gross receipts were fifteen hundred dollars a week. Phineas had pulled it off. When these began to fall he exhibited Joice Heth throughout New England, going from town to town. Joice enjoyed it. She reclined on a couch and smoked a corn-cob pipe throughout the day, and when asked how long she had smoked replied: 'One hundred and twenty years'. In his autobiography Barnum wrote that she told him many things about the Washington family which he had never known before. When business in Boston was not good, Barnum wrote a letter signed 'A Visitor' to one of the newspapers, stating that Joice was a humbug, that she was not real at all, that she was made of india-rubber, whalebone and concealed springs and that her speech was produced by a ventriloquist. Crowds began to arrive, eager to form their own judgment as to whether Joice was real or not. But she was real enough, for she died in February, 1836, and a New York surgeon dissected her corpse and gave it as his opinion, based on the absence of any hardening of the arteries in the heart region, that Joice could not have possibly been more than eighty years of age. The story found its way to the newspapers and Barnum was accused of having invented not only Joice's age but the now obvious nonsense of the Washington background. He did not deny it, and by that, oddly enough, his reputation was greatly enhanced, for many people admired him for fooling them.

Barnum had long been thinking of the circus and now entered into a partnership with Aaron Turner, one of the earliest of American circus proprietors. Turner could never resist a practical joke and one of these nearly had fatal consequences for Barnum. The countryside was full of gossip of a gruesome murder. The Reverend Ephraim K. Avery, accused of the crime, had been acquitted, but it was not a popular verdict for it was widely believed that he was guilty. The circus was at Annapolis, and Turner, drinking with some men in the hotel bar, saw Barnum walking along the street. In a stage whisper he said: 'There goes Avery, the dastardly murderer of Miss Cornell'. No sooner were the words uttered than the bar was deserted and a mob was running after Barnum. He was seized, pinioned, and told that he was about to be tarred and feathered and then hung from the nearest tree. Barnum declared that he was Barnum, not Avery, but the crowd had never heard of Barnum and he had great difficulty in persuading it to take him back to the hotel where, he said, Turner could identify him. Turner looked at him and carelessly remarked that there must be some mistake. 'My friend,' he explained 'has on a new suit of black clothes; it makes him look so like a priest that I mistook him for Avery!'

After a few months the two men parted, and Phineas struck out with a first circus of his own. Just before one performance a Negro singer left without notice, and Phineas, fearful of disappointing his audience, took his place, blacking his face and appearing in the ring to sing coon songs. He was wildly applauded and encored. But his 'Barnum's

The Barnum Museum in New York, opened on 1 January 1842.

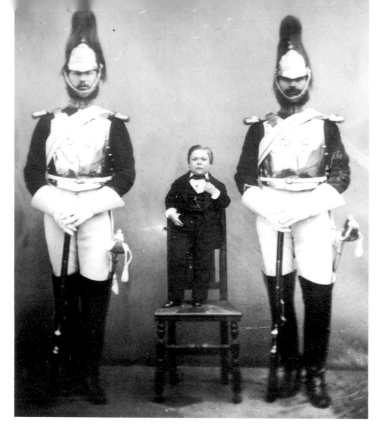

Grand Scientific and Musical Theatre' lost money and he soon had to disband it. Other ventures in travelling showmanship followed, but in 1841 he was back in New York with less money than when he had arrived there five years before. He bought a large stock of illustrated Bibles, opened an office, and appointed agents throughout the State to sell them; but he must have picked a particularly bad lot of salesmen, for they soon cheated him out of profits and capital. He was at the lowest ebb of his fortunes and was reduced to writing advertisements for the Bowery Amphitheatre at a wage of four dollars a week.

Having nothing, he now succeeded in buying the American Museum on credit, one of his master-strokes of astuteness, bluff and cunning. The main security he offered to cover the purchase price was Ivy Island, a solitary tract of bogs and snakes and stunted ivies, which had become a family joke and which had been left to Barnum by his grandfather Phineas. With his usual flare Barnum acquired the existing collection at the Museum which opened under his management on the first day of 1842. He now

Above General Tom Thumb with two Horseguards on a visit to England.

Right General and Mrs Tom Thumb, Commodore Nutt and Miss Minnie Warren.

Opposite A poster advertising the last appearance of Tom Thumb before his departure for America.

Under the distinguished Patronage of
HER MAJESTY, PRINCE ALBERT, THE QUEEN DOWAGER,
THE KING AND QUEEN OF THE FRENCH, THE KING AND
QUEEN OF THE BELGIANS, THE EMPEROR OF RUSSIA, THE
QUEENS OF SPAIN, THE ROYAL FAMILIES AND NOBILITY OF
ENGLAND, FRANCE, BELGIUM AND SPAIN,

and visited during the last two years,

MORE THAN 3,000,000 PERSONS.

GEN.L TOM THUMB

*The American Man in Miniature, 14 years of Age, 25 inches
high, and weighs only 15 pounds, will hold his Farewell Levees*

POSITIVELY FOR *One* DAY ONLY

IN THE *Town Hale Ryde*

On Monday Aug.t 24

previous to his Final Departure for America.

*The little General will appear in his various extra-
ordinary Performances and Costumes, including
Songs, Dances, Ancient Statues, the Napoleon and
Highland Costumes, Citizens Dress, &c. &c.*

HOURS OF EXHIBITION

12 to 2, 3 to 5, & 7 to 9

ADMISSION ONE SHILLING

CHILDREN UNDER TEN YEARS OF AGE HALF PRICE

*The General's Miniature Equipage will promenade the Streets
during   the day.*

THE MAGNIFICENT PRESENTS   RECEIVED FROM THE FIRST

CROWNED HEADS IN THE   WORLD WILL BE EXHIBITED.

G. Webb & Co Litho   Farringdon St London.

exercised all his ingenuity in advertising and publicity, and in a few months every New Yorker was talking of the American Museum – and not only talking but paying good money for admission. Barnum's outstanding exhibit was the Fejee Mermaid. It was a fake, but it deceived. One visitor remarked to Barnum: 'I lived two years on the Fiji Islands and I never heard talk of a mermaid'. 'There's no accounting for some men's ignorance', was Barnum's reply. Besides the Mermaid, Phineas showed living statues, industrious fleas, jugglers, educated dogs, rope-dancers, automatons, albinos, fat boys, giants, gypsies, ventriloquists, knitting machines, models of Dublin, Paris and Jerusalem, glass blowing and dioramas of The Creation, The Deluge and A Storm at Sea. In his first year the profits amounted to nearly twenty-eight thousand dollars and he had established the Museum as a favourite resort.

In 1842 he began his long association with General Tom Thumb which culminated in the highly spectacular wedding of Tom and Lavinia Warren. In 1846 Barnum's fortune was immense, for five years of sensational popularity had made the Museum a gold-mine and the receipts of the Tom Thumb tour had been considerable. Barnum now decided to build a residence befitting his wealth, in which he could reside with Charity and his family. Having purchased seventeen acres of land at Bridgeport on Long Island Sound, he instructed a London architect to draw up the plans for a building in the style of the Pavilion at Brighton, for, while in England, Barnum had seen this polygenetic monument to George IV and had been extremely impressed. Barnum's building, equally exotic and grandiose when finished, was a combination of Byzantine, Moorish and Turkish architecture, with broad piazzas and numerous minarets and spires. The interior was correspondingly fantastic and included a Chinese library with Chinese paintings and furniture. His aim, Barnum had declared, was comfort, and he was satisfied. This costly edifice he named 'Iranistan'.

In 1849, John Hall Wilton, an Englishman travelling the States with the Sax-Horn Players, suggested to Barnum the engagement of Jenny Lind for a series of concerts. The Swedish Nightingale was then at the height of her European fame and had just declared her intention of never again singing in opera, for, after profound reflection on the subject, she had decided that opera was immoral and to appear in it would therefore be contrary to her religious convictions. She was already dallying with other American offers when Wilton, commissioned by Barnum to act as his agent, found her at Lubeck where she had retired to rest. He informed her of Barnum's offer and submitted a draft contract. This was for a hundred and fifty concerts, Jenny Lind to receive a thousand dollars for each one. The contract was signed. Jenny Lind afterwards told Barnum that she had accepted his offer because he was the only manager who had not asked her to share in losses as well as profits, but her chief reason had been her admiration of the engraving of 'Iranistan' which adorned the heading of Barnum's letter paper. She had argued that a gentleman who had been successful enough in business to afford such a palace could not be a mere adventurer. Under Barnum's management during the years 1850-1 she gave ninety-three concerts. Her progress through the States was astonishing. She was talked of as 'the musical wonder of the world' and people fought and scrambled to buy tickets at fabulous prices to hear her sing. Her triumph was all the more astonishing as, before her arrival, her name had been quite unknown in America. If the tour was a triumph for Jenny Lind it was an equal triumph for Barnum and his daring publicity methods which made her name a household word. It was estimated that Barnum netted nearly two hundred thousand dollars before Jenny broke her contract and refused to sing any more. The strain of the protracted tour had been too much for her and in the last few weeks jaded nerves had led to disagreement. When she sang at Philadelphia, for instance, she found that the theatre had been used as a circus for the previous show and she complained that her dressing-room smelt like a stable. She was not a horse, she assured Barnum. But they parted good friends and Jenny always held Barnum in high esteem.

Barnum was now so widely famed that he was given the first offer of freaks and oddities from all over the world. He also paid more for anything he wanted than anyone else. His outstanding weakness, however, persisted; he could never refrain from investing his money in any harebrained schemes which were brought to his attention and he was invariably a loser by these. Outside the show world he was no 'Prince of Humbugs',. but one of those 'suckers' who, he himself declared, were born every minute of every day. In 1855 this tendency resulted in disaster. His affairs with the Jerome Clock Company were complicated and have never been fully unravelled, but

Jenny Lind, 'the Swedish Nightingale'. Her tour of America in 1850 was said to have resulted in a $200,000 profit for Barnum.

when the company became insolvent Barnum was heavily involved and compelled to become a bankrupt, having lost more than half a million dollars. 'Iranistan' was taken over by his creditors. But Tom Thumb came to his rescue and once more he and Barnum toured England. When he was not attending to the General's business, Phineas gave lectures on 'The Art of Money-Getting', the proceeds from which helped to pay his debts so that when he returned to the States he was almost solvent again.

It was not until 1870, when he was sixty, that his name became inseparably connected with the circus. The year before, again a wealthy man, he had decided that the time had now come when he should devote himself 'to serious reflections on the ends and aims of human existence', but he had not got far with these philosophic reflections when they were stampeded by the arrival of W. C. Coup and Dan Costello, two showmen of considerable reputation and experience, with a proposition that Phineas should join them in a travelling circus of ambitious size. Barnum accepted and the venture became the largest he had ever embarked upon. The show opened in 1871 with a tent of colossal proportions and with more men, horses and other animals than any other circus had yet carried. But the great attraction of this first season was the Fiji Cannibals. 'Accompanying them' picturesquely stated the advertising posters 'is a half-civilised Cannibal Woman, converted and educated by Methodist Missionaries. She reads fluently and very pleasantly from the Bible printed in the Fijian language, and she

JUMBO REFUSING TO LEAVE THE ZOO.

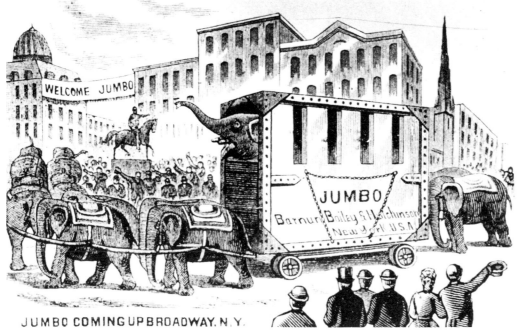

JUMBO COMING UP BROADWAY, N.Y.

Left In 1882 Barnum bought Jumbo the giant elephant from the London Zoo for a thousand dollars. The British public were scandalized and Jumbo was heartbroken. But Barnum, who had a genius for publicity, made sure that Jumbo's arrival in New York was a grand spectacle.

already exerts a powerful moral influence on these Savages . . . They earnestly declare their convictions that eating human flesh is wrong, and faithfully promise never again to attempt it.' In 1872 the show became a two-ring circus; eventually it was to grow into the three-ring circus now universal in America.

In the November of the following year Phineas was in Hamburg when he received a cablegram informing him that Charity was dead. He was heartbroken and particularly angry at being alone in a strange land, separated by four thousand miles from the death-bed of his beloved. He said he would never get over his loss, for never had a man been blessed with such a devoted wife and companion. A year later he married Nancy Fish, the daughter of an English acquaintance.

Meanwhile he returned to America where 'Barnum's Great Moral Show', as his circus was called, was making vast sums for him. His name had now become a legend throughout the land and all who came to the show made a point of seeing him if they could. At Toronto he heard a boy ask: 'Say, Pa, which cage is Barnum in?' On another occasion he sat in his circus behind a farmer and his wife. In the ring a young equestrian was balanced on his head on the back of a galloping horse. The farmer jumped to his feet and shouted in wild excitement: 'I'll bet five dollars that's Barnum. There ain't another man in America who can do that but Barnum!'

These were days of fierce and bitter rivalry between the travelling circuses. Each strove to outdo the other, by no matter what means. One circus company even went to the lengths of burning a railway bridge over which it had just passed, so that a rival show could not get to its next stand. 'Wait for Barnum. Don't spend your money on inferior shows' blarneyed Barnum's circus bills. The greatest rivalry was that between Barnum's Great Moral Show and Howes' Great London Circus, Sanger's Royal British Menagerie, and Grand International Allied Shows, owned by Cooper, James A. Bailey and Hutchinson. A climax was reached when the first elephant ever born in captivity was born on the latter show. Barnum telegraphed an offer of one hundred thousand dollars for it. Bailey refused and printed on his advertising matter a reproduction of Barnum's offer under an enormous caption of 'What Barnum Thinks of the Baby Elephant'. Barnum realised that this cut-throat game could not continue and suggested that the two circuses should be combined. Agreement was reached in 1880, and the two shows now became one, called Barnum and Bailey, The Greatest Show on Earth.

Two years later Barnum pulled off his last great coup. This was the purchase for ten thousand dollars of Jumbo from the London Zoo. It produced a furore of indignation in England and became the most important question of the day. Queen Victoria, the Prince of Wales and Ruskin implored the Zoo to refuse to deliver the elephant, the *Daily Telegraph* cabled Barnum offering to buy back Jumbo at any price, an action in Chancery was brought seeking an injunction against Jumbo leaving the country, thousands of letters were written to the press and a wave of sentimentalism swept the country. It was of no avail. Escorted by Whimsical Walker the clown, Jumbo sailed to America on the 'Assyrian Monarch'. For eighteen months he was exhibited all over the States, the daily takings averaging fifteen thousand dollars. Then a locomotive hit him in the back as he was leisurely walking along a railway track and toppled him down an incline to his death.

Bailey, generally acknowledged to have been the master showman both past and present, introduced a third ring and devised intervening stages. Brilliant alike as an organiser, originator and financial genius, he directed superb productions throughout America and toured European countries at the head of the largest circus ever sent across the Atlantic. In 1888 he informed Phineas that the Greatest Show was going to England. 'That'll cost a lot of money!' he exclaimed. The next year the show was at Olympia. Every afternoon Phineas, now an old man, dressed in a frock-coat, turndown collar, a shirt of many ruffles with a big diamond stud jauntily flashing in the centre, drove round the arena in an open carriage, at intervals stopping to rise to his feet, remove his top hat, and squeak in his high-pitched Yankee voice: 'I suppose you've all come to see Barnum. Wa-al, I'm Barnum.' The Prince of Wales visited the show, and Barnum was presented to him. The Princess of Wales went four times. On the last occasion she asked Barnum to postpone his return to America so that Queen Victoria could see the show. Barnum said he was sorry, he couldn't wait. The Princess had better tell Her Majesty she was making a mistake in not coming before he packed up. Prince George was taken and the future King George V was asked by Barnum where he would be sitting at the end of the performance. The boy looked cautiously around and then said: 'Mr Barnum, I shall

Above 'Freaks, Percy! How dreadful! But it does seem a pity to miss them when they're here.' A magazine cartoon from 1898, relating to the arrival of Barnum and Bailey's show.

Opposite Late nineteenth-century posters from Paris and New York showing acts familiar today, with the exception of the butterfly lady emerging from her chrysalis, who was probably part of a museum of 'living curiosities'.

Overleaf top Poster for Barnum and Bailey's Greatest Show on Earth, showing the variety of acts which could be accommodated in the three rings introduced by Bailey.

Overleaf below Posters advertising the shows of some of their competitors.

Following page A lion-tamer of the last century deliberately tries to evoke the atmosphere of the Roman circus.

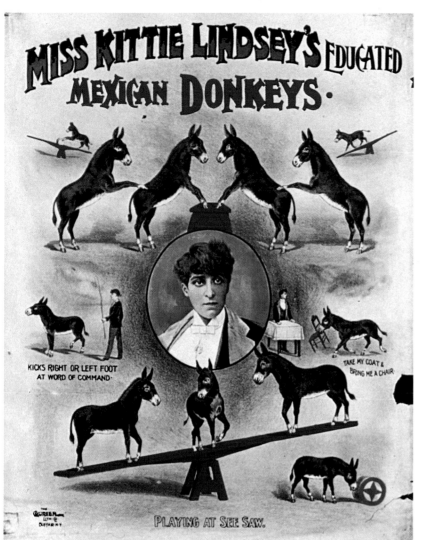

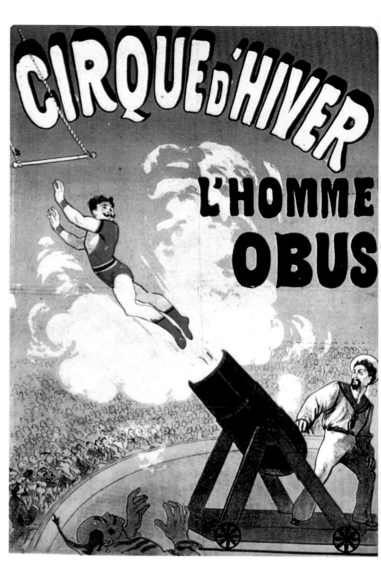

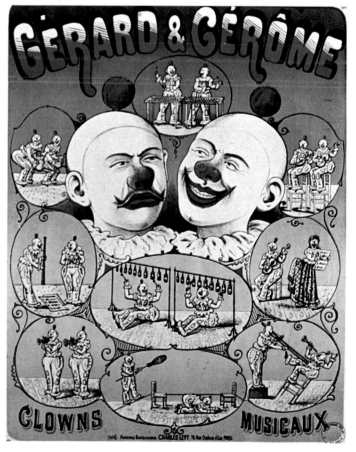

THE BARNUM GREAT

THE BIG SHOW OF THE WORLD

THE MIGHTY CRADOC
IN AN ORIGINAL AND REMARKABLE
PERFORMANCE WITH LARGE
ROMAN AXES.

SELLS BROTHERS
ENORMOUS UNITED SHOWS

COL. W. F. CODY
BUFFALO BILL
THE WORLD FAMOUS SCOUT GUIDE & ORIGINATOR OF THE
GREAT WILD WEST EXHIBITION

&BAILEY
SHOW ON EARTH.

COPYRIGHT 1894 BY THE STROBRIDGE LITH. CO., CIN'TI & NEW YORK.

ANNIE OAKLEY

A SPECIAL FEATURE

BUFFALO BILL'S WILD WEST

THE PEERLESS WING AND RIFLE SHOT

RINGLING BROS
WORLD'S GREATEST SHOWS

THE LORCH FAMILY
EUROPE'S GREATEST ACROBATS
MOST MARVELOUS FEATS EVER SEEN
ENGAGED AT THE HIGHEST SALARY EVER PAID ANY SINGLE ATTRACTION

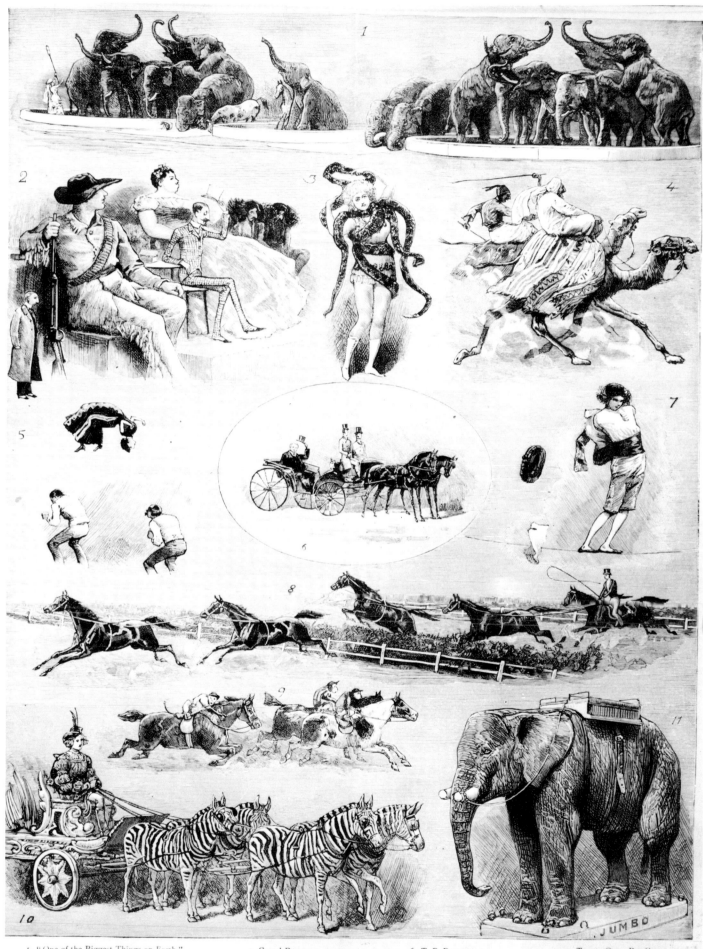

1. "One of the Biggest Things on Earth"
2. "All Sorts and Conditions of Men"
3. The Anaconda Necklace
4. Camel Race
5. "Upon an Even Pedestal with Man"
6. T. P. Barnum
7. "Peeling" on the High Wire
8. The Five-Horse Tandem
9. Two to One—Bar One
10. The Zebra Team
11. "Auld Lang Syne"

SKETCHES AT BARNUM'S SHOW AT OLYMPIA

69

remain here until they play "God Save Grandmother".' One night Barnum sat through a performance by the side of Gladstone, while the Bishop of London is reported to have said: 'Well, goodbye, Mr Barnum. I hope I shall see you in Heaven.' 'You will if you are there,' replied Barnum. He returned to America to face a rumour that the show had done badly. Questioned by a reporter, Barnum admitted it was true, the show had done badly, very badly, and lost money every day. 'Lost money: How?' asked the shocked reporter. 'Turning people away,' said Barnum.

Now eighty years old, his passion for publicity was still strong. He tripped over a rope in the circus, fell, and was slightly bruised. As workmen helped him to his feet, he yelled for the press. 'Tell everybody I've been injured in an accident,' he told the reporters who gathered. For a whole day he kept to his bed chuckling over the newspaper accounts of the seriousness of his injuries. But in November of 1890 he was really ill with an acute congestion of the brain. The doctors said he could not live much longer but he rallied immediately he read a premature obituary of himself in *The New York Evening Sun,* and lived another five months. He died on 7 April 1891. His last words were to enquire what the day's circus receipts had been. He left over four million dollars, having made provision for the continuation of the name of Barnum and Bailey as circus proprietors for the next fifty years. His name is still before the public, the largest show in the States now being known as the Ringling Bros. Circus, Barnum and Bailey.

At an office in the winter quarters of the circus a large packing case was discovered, marked in enormous black letters: 'Not to be opened until after the death of P. T. Barnum.' The circus people conjectured that it contained legacies for them. It did. It was filled with copies of *The Life of P. T. Barnum Written by Himself* with instructions that they were to be distributed among his oldest employees. Was it a last chuckle, a last practical joke?

After the death of Barnum in 1891 the 'Greatest Show on Earth' was maintained by his partner Bailey. Less of a publicist than Barnum he yet had a quality of genius in circus management, in finding and securing performers of merit, and a latent charisma which his lustier partner had overshadowed. Earl Chapin May gives this account of his personality:

> Probably no man in his profession, certainly no circus owner and manager, left more sincere mourners than the thin, little magnate known to millions as James A. Bailey. During his later years he had increased his holdings in Barnum and Bailey Ltd., but had presented thousands of shares to faithful members of his organisation until every veteran was a circus stockholder. Hating personal publicity cordially, he had often distributed $10,000 among his employees and associates at Christmas. He liked to keep his benefactions secret. He once sent $2,000 from Vienna to a man he had not seen for five years but who he heard was down on his luck and needed help.
>
> His infallible memory and attention to detail helped him to great power in the circus world. He seldom raised his voice in talking to employees but what he said was always remembered. He had no familiars in the business but he mingled with his people so informally that he frequently sat on a property box or elephant tub and watched them play poker while he slowly turned a pocket-knife between his right thumb and forefinger and silently chewed on a rubber band. To all troupers at all times he was 'Mr Bailey'. He is still 'Mr Bailey' to those who remember him.
>
> I doubt if he valued his personal power. Certainly he did not anticipate the effect his death would have on Barnum and Bailey Ltd. [He died of erysipelas fifteen years after Barnum.] Its stock rapidly declined from more than $5 to $0.25 a share. His widow was glad to sell her shares. Barnum and Bailey Ltd. gave way to Barnum and Bailey's Greatest Show on Earth, audited not by Englishmen but by Americans and controlled by five of the mature Ringling boys from Baraboo, who also owned Ringling Bros. World's Greatest and the Forepaugh-Sells title and property.

Meanwhile there had risen across the horizon the immense five-pointed star of the Ringling Brothers. The sons of German-Alsatian immigrants who had settled in a little Mississippi riverside town, the quintet of sons worked single-mindedly to send out first a Concert Party 'The Classic and Comic Concert Comp' in which they presented plays and vaudeville acts, while the youngest of them was said to be only aged four. In the entertainment-hungry Mid-West they flourished and succeeded in 1885 in putting out a modest circus programme.

How they fared is indicated in two posters from their beginnings. The first is their own:

Previous page Sketches of acts in Barnum's show at Olympia in 1889, showing the man himself driving round the ring in an open carriage. Gladstone visited the show but Barnum would not wait for Queen Victoria.

Above Barnum amalgamated with James A Bailey, one of his greatest rivals, in 1880. A less flamboyant personality than Barnum, Bailey was a clever businessman and administrator and their combined talents ensured the success of 'The Greatest Show on Earth'.

LAST SIX WEEKS.
BARNUM & BAILEY
GREATEST SHOW ON EARTH.

CHANGE OF PROGRAMME.   CLOSING EXHIBITIONS OF THE GRANDEST & MOST SUCCESSFUL SEASON EVER KNOWN IN OLYMPIA.

FINAL PERFORMANCES in LONDON of the BARNUM & BAILEY Greatest Show on Earth.
Positively Closing the Glorious and Triumphant Sojourn

ON SATURDAY, APRIL 2.

THE ENORMOUS HORSE FAIR SHOWING THE VAST CAVALCADE OF HIGH-CLASS STOCK OWNED & EXHIBITED BY THE GREAT BARNUM & BAILEY SHOW. AN ACTUAL SCENE ON THE GREAT HIPPODROME TRACK. OVER 400 CHOICE THOROUGHBREDS FROM ALL PARTS OF THE WORLD

AND THEN TOURING THE WHOLE OF GREAT BRITAIN.
Travelling the Entire, Mighty, Undivided Show UNDER A DAILY EXPENSE OF £1500, with New Acts and New Features introduced into the already Magnificent and Stupendously large Programme of
THRILLING PERFORMANCES AND GRAND DISPLAYS.
Visiting the Provinces upon its own specially constructed 70 Railway Cars, every car nearly 60 feet long.
NEARLY A FULL MILE OF RAILWAY CARS,
And exhibiting all the myriad wonders under TWELVE ENORMOUS CANVAS PAVILIONS,
One alone of which is double the capacity of Olympia.

LAST SIX WEEKS
Of the Grandest Show ever devised by man.

Last chances of witnessing the Most Magnificent Exhibition, the ingenuity, ability, wealth, and wonderful resources of the
KING OF THE AMUSEMENT WORLD, as set before the bewildered eyes of London.
CHANGE OF PROGRAMME.
NEW ACTS INTRODUCED.   NEW FEATURES PRESENTED.   NEW ATTRACTIONS ADDED.
New Races, new Clown Capers, new Animal Tricks.   Ending the London Engagement in a blaze of glory.   Eye-Feasts of Splendour and Thrilling Interest.   First presentation of the Mammoth
FOUR HUNDRED BLUE RIBBON HORSE FAIR,
And numerous other remarkable features.
A VERITABLE TORNADO OF WONDERS.   BEWILDERING ARRAY OF NOVELTIES,
And a very Vesuvius of Brilliant Attractions never seen here or anywhere else.
A PROGRAMME OF AMAZING EXTENT
Of startling Struggles, hotly contested Races, and Aerial and Equestrian Rivalries, carrying the spectators by storm, and wildly and enthusiastically applauded by everybody.

HIDEOUS HYENA STRIATA GIGANTIUM!
To be Seen Only With the Ringling Show

The Mammoth Midnight Marauding Man-Eating Monstrosity, the Prowling Grave Robbing Demon of all Created Things, who, while the World Sleeps and no hand is raised to stay his awful Depredations, Sneaks Stealthily Under Cover of Darkness to the Cemetery and with Ghoulish Glee Robs the Tomb.

His Hideous Blood-Curdling laughter paralyses with Terror the bravest Hearts. He leaves behind him a trail of Blood, and the Wails of the Dying are Music to his Ear.

The second, produced by a rival company is more revealing, showing as it does the lengths which jealousy could go to, and the freedom from any laws of libel:

When Thieves Fall out Honest Men Get Their Dues.
WARNING!
Neighbors Unchain Your Dogs.
Get Out Your Shotguns.
Keep Your Children at Home.
THE MARAUDERS ARE COMING!   Beware of Them.

Above An advertisement for Barnum and Bailey's circus from the *Illustrated London News*, February 1898.

They Go by The Name of Ringling Brothers.
You Will Know Them By Their Appearance.
They Look Like a Gypsy Camp.
They Are Thieves, Liars and Scoundrels.
They Have No Show Worthy of The Name.
They Sneak From Town to Town Under Cover of Darkness.
They Plunder and Steal Even the Washings Hanging in Back Yards.
We Who Give This Warning Are Also Thieves, But We
Have Fallen Out With The Greasy Pack and
Now Tell The Truth.

In spite of such attacks and all the misfortunes of a tenting circus everywhere, blow-downs, punch-ups, animals poisoned or ailing, the five young men continued and bought two elephants, a springboard in every circus's history. They had Jules Turnour, one of the greatest of clowns, on their bill and a big top seating 4,000 people until they were large enough to absorb the Greatest Show on Earth. Their immense world-thundering show was literally too large to come to Europe but became in name synonymous with all that is 'circus' in the United States.

But the brothers did not remain as a single entity directing 'The Ringling Brothers and

Right A French poster advertising the freaks at Barnum and Bailey's circus. Amongst the more exotic curiosities are a bearded lady, and a man with elastic skin.

Barnum and Bailey's Greatest Show on Earth'. One by one they dropped away, selling out their shares to the remaining brothers till only John, universally called 'Mr John' remained the sole proprietor of the vast concern, a strange man who looked like a bulldog, was an art-collector as well as a millionaire circus-owner and director who never forgot the 'director's' duty to his inheritance and achievement.

From the days of Astley in London and John Bill Ricketts in Philadelphia the British and American circuses have always enjoyed liaison, competition and the tendency to out-boast one another, but they were never brought together in a more dramatic way than in the love-affair (if that is the word) between the English poet Algernon Charles Swinburne and the American circus rider, Adah Isaacs Menken.

In the 1860s before Swinburne came under the tutelage of Theodore Watts-Dunton, he was leading a curiously undisciplined life in London. One can see him in dingy lodgings, known always as 'my chambers', surrounded by antimacassars, festooned mantelpieces, heavy pieces of furniture, propped on a horsehair sofa declaiming to his friends, while the only things of any beauty in sight were his books. He did not collect the paintings of the artists he knew as he might so easily have done, but was in his private life without much taste in furniture, food, dress, music or the lesser arts. He does

Freaks were always a major attraction of Barnum's shows and he was prepared to pay the highest prices for human curiosities from all over the world.

73

not seem to have cared about typography or binding. So there he would squat perkily in his ill-tailored long-wearing suits, proclaiming in uncontrolled ecstasy the glories of de Sade, Mazzini, Landor, Blake – any of his heroes.

Or emerging after nightfall into a London scarcely changed from that, a freakish figure with his red hair and skipping walk, he would make his way perhaps a little uncertainly to the house of one of his friends from which he would have to be brought home in a cab. Even in the harsh gas-light he would be noticeable, his short legs, his violent tic, his wasted haunted look, while sometimes on that mass of hair a tall hat was balanced.

He would be invited to 'breakfast' somewhere and would be either taciturn at table or far too talkative. The telegraph system had not yet (till 1870) been taken over by the post office and everything was done by messages sent by hand, invitations replied to while the bearer waited. All too often Swinburne would fail to appear after accepting, and write repentant letters next day explaining the 'illness' which had prevented him. He subscribed to most of the important reviews and weeklies and scoured the pages of the daily press for items which tickled his erotic fancy, being rewarded in April 1860 by an account of a pupil being beaten to death by a schoolmaster. He would trip round to the British Museum Reading Room for some piece of research and write long letters full of facetious references to flagellation. Most grotesquely of all he would walk from his rooms in Dorset Street through Regent's Park, stopping at a bench occasionally to scribble, on his way to St John's Wood where in a discreet house two obliging women, described as 'golden-haired and rouge-cheeked' were paid to chastise him. He spoke of this as a *'maison de supplices à la Rodin'* (a reference to de Sade's *Justine*), as 'the Grove of the Beloved Disciple', and as 'the Sadice-Paphian spring of St John's Wood'. The picture of Swinburne, in frock coat and top hat, attending there is tragi-comic, but his visits

Below The immigrant Ringling family in 1894, some years after they had established themselves as entertainers in the Mid-West.

The five Ringling brothers put on their first modest circus programme in 1885. Eventually they took over the Greatest Show on Earth and today 'Ringling Brothers, Barnum and Bailey's' is the best known circus in America.

came to an end after a monetary dispute with the two ladies.

There is some mystery about a friend of Swinburne's called John Thomson, but if we could accept him as a cynical bawdy-house keeper there would be no difficulty about believing that he introduced Swinburne to Adah Isaacs Menken, so eliminating an improbable story that the meeting between Swinburne and the circus rider was the result of an earnest family conference called by Dante Rossetti who thought it would 'make a man' of Swinburne.

Menken was a grand creature physically, no longer very young and never very beautiful but with limbs called by her admirers 'statuesque'. She was born Dolores McCord, but the first of her five marriages was to a Jewish music-master Alexander Isaacs Menken and she kept his name which she used on the title-page of the pamphlets of verse she had printed. She had been actress, model and provincial *salonnière* but never openly a prostitute, and had travelled a great deal in the States and Europe. She had a special predilection for writers and in 1866 had a notorious affair with Alexandre Dumas the elder.

At the time she met Swinburne she was working a profitable racket in both the theatre and circus. Billed as 'The Naked Mazeppa' she wore pink tights and had herself strapped to the back of a horse which ambled round circus ring or stage. The link with Byron – the act had originally started as a melodrama adapted from Byron by H. M. Milnes – was not appreciated by most of the audience, but its name caught the Victorians in their thousands and suggestive posters did the rest. The Americans had accorded Menken resounding and profitable applause for her daring – not so much in being jolted round a ring upside down but in using that title and appearing in flesh-coloured tights, and she had been encouraged to bring her act to Europe. She appeared in London at Astley's in 1864 and 1865, crossed several times to Paris, returned to the States and appeared in London again in 1866 and 1867, always repeating her performance. It was in the autumn of this last year that Swinburne met her, perhaps through the Pre-Raphaelites who thought her a 'stunner', perhaps through John Thomson, or perhaps by his own volition.

She appears to have been a kindly, vulgar, not unintelligent creature with a passion for literature and literary men. Her own verse was lachrymose and deplorable but she was proud of it and felt her noisy reputation as a circus rider robbed her of the eminence due to her as a poetess. Swinburne was just what she wanted, a famous man of letters who appeared to adore her.

Perhaps he did, in some mystical totemistic way of his own. For here she was in person, his Belle Dame Sans Merci, his superwoman, his Dolores. With her lavish

Right The statuesque Adah Menken as she appeared in her circus act.

Below The poet Swinburne photographed with his 'mistress', the American trick-rider Adah Menken. She wrote bad poetry and liked literary lovers.

Opposite Part of Toulouse-Lautrec's series of pastels devoted to the circus.

physique and her acceptance of the applause of multitudes she must have seemed to him his pitiless goddess.

Besides, he was proud of his achievement in attracting her attention. A photograph was taken of them together, with the circus lady in costume sitting on a chair, and little Swinburne standing beside her wearing a frock-coat and trying not to look diminutive. It is irresistibly funny, but both were proud of their association and circulated the picture so much among their friends that it was mentioned in the press and caused perturbation to Admiral Swinburne and his wife. Poet and equestrienne seem to have spent a good deal of time together, including several whole nights, but without any satisfactory result, Menken reporting to Dante Rossetti that she 'hadn't been able to get him up to scratch', and adding plaintively, 'I can't make him understand that biting's no good.'

It is improbable that she spoke in these earthy terms to Swinburne himself, for when he had one of his falls from a hansom cab and damaged his face so much that he kept away from her, Thomas Purnell reported to Swinburne:

Today I have had a letter from Dolores – such a letter! She fears you are ill; she is unable to think of anything but you; she wishes me to telegraph to her if you are in danger, and she will fly on the wings of the wind to nurse you. She has become a soft-throated serpent, strangling prayers on her white lips to kiss the poet, whose absence leaves her with ghosts and shadows. She concludes: 'Tell him all – say out my despairing nature to him – take care of his precious life. Write at once; believe in me and my holy love for him. Let him write one word in your letter. He will, for he is so good!'

Swinburne, on the other hand, spoke of her in letters as he spoke of other obsessions, like the flogging-block, with facetious humour.

'I must send you in a day or two', he wrote with cock-a-hoop satisfaction to Powell, 'a photograph of my present possessor – known to Britannia as Miss Menken, to me as Dolores (her real Christian name) – and myself taken together.' The 'present' possessor, with its naive attempt at the blasé, is revealing.

UNPRECEDENTED SUCCESS
OF
MISS ADAH ISAACS
MENKEN

AS MAZEPPA!
Which will be Performed every Evening until further notice.

RINGLING BROS AND BARNUM & BAILEY COMBINED SHOWS

THE WORLD'S MOST TERRIFYING LIVING CREATURE!

GARGANTUA THE GREAT
THE LARGEST AND FIERCEST GORILLA EVER BROUGHT BEFORE THE EYES OF CIVILIZED MAN!

Menken died in Paris in the following year and Swinburne's words (in a letter to Powell) have been frequently quoted: 'I am sure you were sorry on my account to hear of the death of my poor dear Menken – it was a great shock to me and a real grief – I was ill for some days. She was most lovable as a friend as well as a mistress.' To read too much into the last word would be to gain a false impression. It may have been inserted for bravado, or 'mistress' may have had some special meaning for Swinburne derived from his obsessions. The whole abortive affair lasted only a few weeks and, although Menken has been foolishly called 'the only woman in Swinburne's life', and romanticised with other turgid phrases such as might have been quoted from her own verse, she was in fact a striptease artist a century before her time, the ex-wife of a number of sordid characters including a booth boxer, and her sentimental yearning after literature and poets bored Swinburne, who told Gosse that she woke him up early in the morning and insisted on reading her poetry to him, swinging her handsome legs on the edge of the bed. She may have obliged him by some Sadic pantomime; she certainly could not obtain – as she complained to Rossetti – any normal response from him. But Adah Menken earned a certain place in the biography of one who must certainly be called a great English poet.

No account of the American circus would be complete without the name of 'Buffalo Bill', and with that name those of Annie Oakley, Sitting Bull and Wild Bill Hickock. He was William Cody, a showman who organised and made an occasional success of his Wild West Show in London and Paris, as well as in the States. It is difficult to untangle the thin line of fact that runs through his life-story but it appears that for the first thirty years of his life Cody lived the haphazard, precarious and turbulent life of the West in the 1860s and 1870s. During those years he helped negroes to escape from the cotton plantations, saw his father mortally knifed, was a boy rider of a Pony Express, saw service with the Union Army both as a scout and a spy, fought in the Indian wars, was waylaid by Redskins, ambushed by bandits and shot at by mail thieves. He also achieved wide fame as a slayer of buffaloes on the grand scale. As early as 1870, when Cody was a mere twenty-four, Ned Buntline (Edward Z. C. Judson) wrote a fantastic account of his

Left A poster for Astley's circus advertising Adah Menken as Mazeppa, Byron's heroine. Her flesh-coloured tights caused a sensation at Astley's in 1864 and 1865.

Above Poster featuring Gargantua the Gorilla, 1938.

Opposite top *Parade de Cirque* by C. Lagar, 1920. Petit Palais, Geneva.

Opposite bottom *Les Musiciens* by C. Lagar, 1930. Petit Palais, Geneva.

adventures called *The King of Bordermen,* which still sells. It was the forerunner of a vast literature in which Cody figures as hero. Fact and fiction became for a long time indistinguishable, for Buffalo Bill's adventures went on week after week as indefatigably as Billy Bunter's. The output of dime periodicals and penny dreadfuls in which he appeared was prodigious. One author alone, Prentiss Ingraham, who claimed to have shared the blanket and camp-fire of his hero, wrote 203 Buffalo Bill thrillers, and these are still published and read in America. Some authors, in order to convey a false verisimilitude, a suggestion that their narratives were written by men whose lives were similar to that of Cody, adopted names such as might have been borne by hard-bitten Westerners, among them Nebraska Ned and Harry Hawkeye. At first Cody read these productions with a mingling of surprise and amusement. 'Gosh! What they say!' he exclaimed. But he made no protest or move to contradict them. He knew it was all excellent publicity for his Wild West Show. When he was a man of nearly seventy he remarked to Charles Hamid, the American entertainment promoter: 'I read in a book lately that I shot 4,280 buffaloes in eighteen months. Sounds like a lot of bison meat. Well, perhaps I did!' He began to put his own name to these amusing and incredible romances. It seems unlikely that a man of his limited literacy actually wrote them or had much contact with those who did so; if he had, perhaps the wilder statements would have been edited before publication, though he wrote to one publisher saying: 'I have really gone a bit far this time!' 'When it comes to writing of myself,' he says in one of his numerous 'autobiographies', 'I am staggered.'

When his Wild West Show was being watched by hundreds of thousands of people in England and America, the legend grew. His publicity agents wrote startling accounts of his life and adventures, which were published in the programmes or sold in book form to audiences. A play was even issued in the English toy theatre 'Penny Plain, Tuppence Coloured', Cody thus jostling shoulders in juvenile popularity with the famous pirates and highwaymen and such notorieties as Sweeney Todd, George Barnwell and Guy Fawkes. The sheets were published in 1887 with the title of *Buffalo Bill's Wild West Ride* in a 'Penny Packet' by Clark of Manchester.

Poster advertising 'the world's largest, grandest, best amusement institution'.

In the late nineties, the Aldine Company published many stories said to have been written by Cody. In these he scalped Indians – 'Buffalo Bill shouted in ringing tones: "The first scalp for Custer!"' He was depicted with hags in haunted canyons and spectral riders who galloped across the plains with phosphorescent hounds at their heels (thus anticipating Conan Doyle's *The Hound of the Baskervilles*). One story begins gruesomely with a description of the heroine opening a parcel which has been given to her, to find that it contains her lover's scalp and eyeballs. In others, Cody rescues 'old pards' as a matter of routine, whether they are about to be crushed to death by bears, drowned in rapids or shot by Indians. Sometimes he is bound, like Byron's Mazeppa, to the back of a mustang, and when his clothes are soaked in kerosene he is sent flying across the plains like a blazing torch. Often he is captured by Redskins and threatened with torture. Bound to a stake, he faces a circle of braves who are about to throw the knives they hold ready, but his mesmeric eyes always quell the knife-throwers to inaction. When not fighting Indians, he is hunting buffaloes or horse thieves or arriving 'in the nick of time' to rescue innocent men from lynching. Always he is in the right place at the right moment, and always escaping death by what can only be described as a miracle.

The Wild West Show, in the making of which Cody spent the last half of his life, was a projection of himself on the grand scale, for Cody was one of those blessed born innocents who never really grow up. His early life was truly adventurous, dangerous, even heroic, and he never outlived his love for the excitements of his youth. Play-acting, riding, shooting with his Wild West Show was all he could do to perpetuate the zest of boyhood, and he did it with a gusto that made the show itself a legend.

Like the old-time circuses, his show always paraded through a town. Cody would ride at the head, preceding the bullet-spattered Deadwood Coach and his magnificent troupe, with its lumbering line of wagons, imposing groups of feathered Redskins in full war-paint, whooping cowboys on bucking broncos, and squaws, papooses, herds of buffalo, mustangs and dogs. His was the most imposing figure of all. Almost six feet in height, with the head of a stage musketeer, his greying hair fell from under a Stetson hat

Queen Victoria visits the Wild West Show at West Brompton in 1887.

81

The legendary figure of Buffalo Bill. Fed by
stories of his true-life exploits, audiences
on both sides of the Atlantic loved his
show, a precursor of the modern Western.

and curled luxuriantly about his shoulders. His brown eyes had the clear, steady gaze of the marksman; the straight classical nose was that of the old-time American frontiersman. His attire for these occasions was a hunting shirt made of deerskin, beautifully dressed and tanned, long leggings of the same material, the broad collar and leg seams decorated with bright-hued fringes; he wore moccasins on his feet, around his middle was buckled a leather belt in which, besides ammunition pouches, were stuck a hatchet and a hunting-knife.

Also riding among his warrior troupe was his female star, the grim-looking Annie Oakley. Her face when she was in her thirties had hard lines and thin lips, which suggested the prim and dominating schoolmistress; she was billed as 'the infallible little shot,' and dressed in calf-high and scalloped boots, shirt and cowboy skirt, with a flopping sombrero on her head. She was also a child of the frontier, where it was said her name was as much feared as a bullet from her gun. An amazing shot, she had accomplished seeming wonders. Once, at Tiffin, Ohio, she had hit a fifty-cent piece held between a man's finger and thumb from a distance of thirty feet. In February, 1885, handicapped by having to load her own guns, she fired at 5,000 glass balls thrown into the air to a height of forty-five feet by three projectors. In the space of nine hours she broke 4,772 of them. Sceptics explain this extraordinary feat by saying that she used spread shot and that she could hardly miss with spreading bullets. It may be so. At the time her shooting was accepted without a murmur, and it is presumed that her guns

One of the star attractions of the Wild West Show was Annie Oakley of 'Annie Get Your Gun' fame, here looking rather demure.

A group of the original Wild West Company in 1884 showing some of the magnificent Red Indians which formed part of the company.

were examined by those experts present. Certainly no one would dare to call her a faker to her face. Later someone said that of Cody, but although in his last years he lost some of his sureness, in his prime he was Annie Oakley's equal. Johnny Baker, his adopted son, saw him split the edge of a playing-card with a rifle bullet, and Mrs Cody used to be terrified when he shot coins out of the fingers of his children.

Even today the Wild West act is a never-failing attraction at fairs or as an *entrée* in the circus ring. And the performers who crack the bull-whips, coil the ropes, show prowess as dead shots with a rifle, or throw knives and tomahawks round a girl standing against a frame with such precision that the weapons outline her figure, invariably let their hair grow long, cultivate a beard and imitate in their make-up and dress the appearance of Buffalo Bill. Small boys, garbed in feathered head-dress, still play at Red Indians and act the feats of the famous scout.

Cody's great show has passed, like the other great shows of Astley, Barnum and Lord George Sanger, but the memory of it remains curiously alive in the minds of many. And the name of Cody, Buffalo Bill, as a hero of the young may never quite die.

Above William Cody, alias Buffalo Bill, in an open carriage in his later years.

Left Cody featured as the hero of much popular literature. Ned Buntline wrote of his adventures in *Scouts of the Prairie* and *King of Bordermen.*

January 31st, and February 1st.

NED BUNTLINE'S

GREAT REALISTIC DRAMA. THE

SCOUTS OF THE PRAIRIE

INTRODUCING THE

Genuine Western Heroes

BUFFALO BILL
TEXAS JACK,
NED BUNTLINE,
TEN INDIAN WARRIORS,

THE GREAT DANSEUSE

M'LLE MORLACCHI,

AND FULL DRAMATIC COMPANY.

NED BUNTLINE'S SENSATIONAL DRAMA OF

SCOUTS OF THE PRAIRIE,

BUFFALO BILL, by the original Hero, ... Hon. W. F. CODY
TEXAS JACK, by original Hero, ... J. B. OMOHUNDRO
CALE D RG, ... NED BUNTLINE
Mormon Ben, ... Mr Wentworth
Phelim O Laugherty .... Harry Gilbert

The Parade Goes By

While we salute the historic figures of the traditional stationary circuses in Paris, London, Leningrad and, indeed, in all the capitals of Europe and in the great cities in America, it must be remembered that for many, perhaps most people scattered over the map of the civilised world, the circus has no permanent home, but is an exciting event which breaks into their lives with colour, sound and wonder, and is gone again, miraculously, before the countryman's day is fairly commenced. As soon as the crowd of spectators goes out of the great tent after the last performance it is not long before the circus men, performers, bandsmen, and tenants alike have begun and completed the hard work of 'pulling down' and 'packing up' the tents, the seating, the props and cages and all that is left on the 'tober' (circus ground) is a paper bag or two and a few cigarette packets, while the circus is built up for the next day's performance five, ten or fifty miles away. That is tenting, the only life that circus folk know from April to November while they live in their trailers, set round the big top.

The name of the showman who first thought of a tent remains unknown. Sir Robert Fossett had a theory that it derived from the mumming booths and that the first circus tent must have been devised by a sailor: 'the very act of raising the neck of the tent up to the king pole savours largely of the hoisting of the mainsail of a ship up the mast.'

In 1830 there were at least eight well-known circuses on the road: Holloway's, Milton's, Wild's, Bannister's, Saunders's, Cooke's, Samwell's and Clarke's. These early tenting shows travelled with only three or four horses, of which two appeared in the ring. There was usually a show front, imposing and gaudily painted; on its platform the artists and horses paraded to attract the crowd, an acrobat showing his skill, a white-faced clown cracking jokes with the rustics, the showman himself incessantly beating a drum or a gong and shouting 'Walk up! Walk up!' changing to: 'All in, now to begin! All in, now to begin!' The horses would be led or ridden down the platform steps and taken to the side entrance, to emerge again this way, when the show was ended, and resume their places on the platform. Each performance was of short duration and repeated from noon until midnight and as often as the tent could be filled. Receipts were governed by a fickle climate, and then, as now, the life of a tenting circus was one of ups and downs and unremitting effort. There were still those who travelled without the friendly shelter of canvas and gave their performances in the open air, in a meadow or on a common, sometimes at crossroads and in the market-place. In the tent circuses, a ring was cut out of the field and the turves piled to make the ring fence, and the audience stood behind a wooden barrier. There were no seats and the only illumination was that of candlelight, the candles being balanced on pieces of wood held by nails to the side poles, so that their grease dropped on to the heads and shoulders of the audience.

Lord George Sanger described some of the difficulties his father had as a travelling showman:

The old custom had always been for the showmen to draw into the town to take up their pitches the day before the fair. But authorities had come into power who did not recognize old customs, and who, moreover, desired as one of them said, 'to keep the vagabond showmen in their place'.

The Mayor of Warminster, who was a man of very narrow opinions, looked upon show people as little better than emissaries of the Evil One, and resolved to harass them accordingly. He had been told by his clerk, or some other wiseacre, that if the showmen drew into the town the night before the fair and slept in their caravans, as the latter were in no sense houses, they could be arrested for the atrocious crime of 'sleeping out', and so dealt with as 'rogues and vagabonds'.

My father on this particular night had, therefore, no sooner got warm in bed in his caravan, which lay on the outskirts of the fair, than down came the beadle of the parish with his three-cornered hat and gilt staff and two assistants and arrested him. They also from an adjoining caravan took Richard Hunter, who had a travelling museum, and then conveyed their two protesting prisoners to the lock-up.

The next morning they were brought before the Bench and duly charged with sleeping out as against the 'statute made and provided'. The mayor, who presided, read them a long lecture on the iniquity of their calling, and said that in order to show the other caravan dwellers the pains and penalties their 'irregular' mode of life rendered them liable to he had resolved to treat the prisoners as 'rogues and vagabonds' and they would be sentenced to twenty-one days' hard labour each.

Here was an example of justices' justice with a vengeance, but my brave old dad was equal to the occasion.

'Stop a minute, your worship,' he said, 'stop a minute! You have no power to send us to prison, for we were not trespassing, and were sleeping under a roof. In my case, too, I carry the Royal Prescription allowing me to get my living as I choose, providing I do it honestly. I'm only a poor showman, but I know the law, and you will have to pay for this outrage.'

One or two of the other justices looked rather uncomfortable at this, but the mayor said, 'Pooh! What is your word worth? What's this nonsense about a Royal Prescription, eh?'

At this my father pulled out a little waterproof bag which he always carried hung round his neck by a cord, and, opening it, took out a parchment.

'Here,' said he, 'is the document. I served his late Majesty King William for ten long years as a sailor, and was with Nelson on the 'Victory' at Trafalgar. When I left, I got ten pounds a year pension and this parchment, which, amongst other things, says: "James Sanger, as aforesaid, having so done service for His Majesty in the wars with France, is hereby privileged and entitled to carry on any trade, craft or profession whereby he may

Carriages passing the entrance of Barnum's Museum in New York.

87

Right A travelling circus in France. Acrobats who will be performing inside the tent display themselves on the show front, while a drummer and a barker whip up the anticipation of the crowd.

Below Horses from Hengler's Circus salute Queen Victoria in the Royal Box at Windsor.

honestly provide for himself, in any manner he may consider suitable to the needs of the said trade, craft or profession".'

The document further went on to give the holder certain exemptions and travelling rights, and to declare that those interfering with those rights might incur certain penalties. After it had been handed to the justices and perused by them, it was given back to my father, and the mayor said: 'I have never before seen such a document. I cannot say whether it is yours or not, but I will give you the benefit of the doubt. You ought to go to gaol, both of you, but this time you may go away.'

So father, and Hunter with him, both went free, and did very well at the fair, in spite of the mayor's attempt to interfere with them. They afterwards consulted a lawyer to see if they could get any compensation for their arrest, but the man of law advised them to let well alone, as it would cost a lot of money to bring an action, the result of which, even if they gained it, would hardly be likely to pay them for their trouble.

The two brothers completed preparations for separate circuses. George heard that John's was to be called 'John Sanger and Son' (it should have been Sons – John was the father of four boys, all of whom became circus celebrities). George had no son, so lettered on his wagons 'George Sanger and Daughters'. Then one spring morning (it was in the 1870s), a crowd of people gathered outside Astley's. Stretched along the road as far as the eye could see was a long, and apparently never-ending, stream of newly-painted and gaudy wagons and caravans, hundreds of horses and wild-beast cages. Half was George's circus, the other half John's. The time came to make a start, the two brothers

Above Miss Hengler, an equestrienne of class.

Left Poster for Hengler's 'Grand Cirque'.

89

shook hands and wished each other luck. Whips cracked, the two shows moved off, John turning to the north, George to the south. Soon the two circuses were out of sight and sound; twelve years passed before they again met on the road, when there ensued an intense rivalry which only came to an end when the two circuses fought a pitched battle at Wolverhampton.

Even as a boy George had always been referred to as 'His Lordship'. He took great pride in his appearance and when the peepshow gave way to the conjuring booth, George appeared in Hamlet costume – black velvet tunic blazoned with black bugles, a hat of the same material adorned with three enormous ostrich feathers and velvet-topped Hessian boots. He spent an hour daily curling his long hair. The role of a circus proprietor demanded more dignity and for the last forty years of his life he was invariably seen in public dressed in a long-tailed black coat with velvet collar, while a thick gold chain from which was suspended a giant fob stretched across his waistcoat; he wore a flower in his lapel, a silk handkerchief peeped from his breast pocket and his tie was invariably white. Surmounting this was a top hat.

George Sanger elevated himself to the peerage when he fell foul of the famous Buffalo Bill. The two met in the law courts where George had to follow the Honourable William Cody in the witness-box. George got the better of the encounter and with his usual flair for publicising his successes had a handbill printed with the details of the case. While preparing this and referring to the evidence to refresh his memory he became irritated by the constant repetition of 'The Honourable' in front of Cody's name. 'Dang it!' he suddenly exclaimed, 'I can do better than that. If he's an Honourable then I'm ''Lord'' George Sanger from this time on.' He was, and 'George Sanger and Daughters' took the grandiloquent name of 'Lord George Sanger's Circus'.

The effect of this on the other circus proprietors of the time was amusing. John Sanger, not to be outdone by his brother, also became a Lord; Cooke became Sir John

Performances of Sanger's tenting circus in a country town were great events.

V. *R.*

Balmoral Castle, 17th June, 1898.

Lord George Sanger's Circus Company.

BY SPECIAL COMMAND
OF
Her Most Gracious Majesty Queen Victoria.
PERFORMANCE COMMENCING AT 3.30.

...PROGRAMME...

1. Overture by the Magnificent Band. Conductor, E. Scholz.

Henry Cooke, Bob Fossett was transformed into Sir Robert Fossett, and the acrobat head of one of the smallest of the tenting shows went one better than all of them and styled himself King Ohmy! Lion tamers became Captains, and even grooms hinted at aristocratic connections.

In the summer of 1899 George received a command to appear before Queen Victoria at Windsor Castle with all his horses, wild beasts, wagons and chariots. The Queen, sitting in her carriage, was so delighted with the parade that she had to see it all again. George was presented to her.

'So you are Mr Sanger,' the Queen said.

'Yes, Your Majesty,' George replied.

Then, with a smile, the Queen added: 'Lord George Sanger, I believe?'

'Yes, if Your Majesty pleases,' George managed to stammer.

'Very amusing,' remarked the Queen, 'but I hear that you have borne the title very honourably.'

George toured his 'Greatest Show on Earth' all over Europe, and gave Disraeli a magnificent reception at the railway station at Verviers when that statesman was triumphantly returning from the Congress of Berlin of 1878. It was even said that the showman suggested to Disraeli that cynical catch-phrase 'peace with honour' which he flung with such effect in the House when he faced the Opposition.

The latter half of the nineteenth century saw the tenting circuses at the height of their glamour and popularity. In those days the names of Sanger, Hengler, Ginnett and Bostock were household words, and the coming of a circus was a red-letter day in any village or town, the streets of which were always thronged for the slow procession of the circus parade.

Lord George prided himself on his parade; it must have been a grand sight. There was a mirrored tableau, a wagon weighing ten tons with carved and gilded woodwork, drawn by thirty cream horses; the Britannia tableau, three tiers high, surmounted by Mrs George Sanger arrayed as was Britannia on a penny, holding with her left hand a shield painted with the colours of the Union Jack, and with her right, a golden trident. A Greek helmet crowned her head; crouched at her feet were Nero the lion and a lamb. This was followed by a string of camels, a herd of elephants, two hundred and fifty historical characters on horseback, and a great chariot which contained the band who blew furiously into their brass instruments. Angels, sirens, sea-gods and mermaids sported on the sides of the chariot among foamy seas and palm-fringed coral reefs; its gilding glittered in the sun while the bandsmen were magnificent in uniforms of white and gold. This chariot was drawn by forty horses, ten teams, four abreast. Finally came the cages of the wild beasts, grooms leading zebras, llamas and ostriches, and the performers in their ring costumes mounted on prancing thoroughbreds.

A silk programme for the command performance of Sanger's circus at Balmoral in 1898. Queen Victoria enjoyed the show so much that they appeared at Windsor the following year.

Life and Adventures

(AT HOME AND ABROAD)

OF

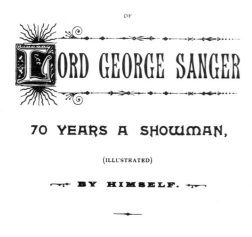

LORD GEORGE SANGER

70 YEARS A SHOWMAN,

(ILLUSTRATED)

BY HIMSELF.

PRICE SIXPENCE.

Published by GEORGE SANGER, London, Margate, and Ramsgate.
Printed by STAFFORD & CO., Netherfield, Notts.

Right Lord George Sanger who was famous for his elegant attire.

Above The title-page of Lord George Sanger's autobiography.

But Lord George was not to die peacefully. He sold his circus and most of his animals at public auction. It was an astonishing sale. If an old-time performer bid for a horse, Sanger would cry: 'Let him have it, he used to ride it!' Sanger was now seventy-eight, beginning to feel old, missing intolerably the companionship of his wife, upon whom he had always rather pathetically depended. Since her death his old fire and zest for the publicity and the excitement of the circus had died too. When he had married her she was the star of George Wombwell's Menagerie, 'Madame Pauline de Vere, the Lady of the Lions' (to be succeeded by her cousin who was killed almost immediately by her favourite tiger). Her task had not been easy, for George was a great showman but a poor business man. He was careless with money and had a horror of book-keeping; indeed, there never was any book-keeping on the Sanger show in those happy days. His wife always handled the money and looked after the business side of the circus, and for that George was deeply grateful.

On one occasion when he arrived home at Margate he suddenly remembered he had left a bag under the seat in the waiting-room at the railway station. A man was sent to fetch it; when he returned his face was streaming with perspiration and he remarked that the bag was very heavy. 'Yes,' said George, 'it would be. There's over £500 in it.'

George often designed the dresses for his spectacles, and would even cut them out if the wardrobe mistress did not understand his ideas. He loved to sit for hours sewing spangles on to the costumes. He was deeply religious, yet when angered by the slowness of his tentmen would swear fluently at them. 'God damn your eyes!' was his favourite expression but he would qualify the blasphemy by adding, 'God forgive me for swearing!'

With a fortune of £30,000, Lord George retired to Park Farm, East Finchley. One Tuesday evening, at the end of November 1911, he was sitting in front of his fire with Harry Austin, one of his old performers, who had just left hospital. Austin was reading aloud from the newspaper when suddenly they were interrupted and startled by the appearance of Herbert Cooper, a recent employee of Sanger, who imagined he had a grievance against Austin. Cooper attacked Austin with an axe and felled him with a blow. A second blow caught Sanger on the temple; the old showman toppled backwards, his head hit the brass fender, and he must have died instantly. For days the newspapers were full of the affair; Lord George had died in a blaze of publicity which would have been sweet to him in his circus days. Interest continued until the murderer's body was found in a railway cutting near Highgate, while Harry Austin miraculously recovered.

Lord George Sanger took his place in his last parade in pouring rain. Bare-headed crowds silently watched the funeral cortège pass from Finchley to Holborn Viaduct Station. At Margate, where he was buried, the shops closed, blinds were drawn and the cabbies tied black bows to their whips. The whole town went into mourning.

Another of these early tenting-circus proprietors was John Clarke, who was often obliged to sell his tent and play in the open air, and instead of making a collection sold tickets at a shilling each for a 'lucky bag'. Prizes were plated teapots, milk jugs, workboxes, japanned teatrays and silk handkerchiefs. He was a great character, always known as Old John, and when he was seventy he was recognised as the father of the equestrian profession and had a circus at the Lambeth Baths in Westminster Bridge Road. To his performers throughout his life he continually pleaded bad times and asserted: 'I shall be ruined, my boys!' His language was ornamented with strange swear words and his sayings and doings became household words among circus artists. 'Ah, my boy! I'm glad to see you. What are you doing? Don't open your mouth too wide, and I may do something for you.' 'Yes, Mr Clarke,' the performer in search of employment would reply. 'I can join you for . . . .' and would name what seemed to him reasonable and moderate terms. In reply Old Clarke would roar: *'Do you want to ruin me?'* Eccentric, but kind-hearted, he was soon relenting if he thought his treatment had been harsh. When he made money he paid his artists, when he lost he considered they should share in his failures. At the Lambeth Baths, where he gave three performances nightly,

Left Poster advertising Sanger's travelling circus, with a space left blank for the venue.

Above Franconi, the French circus proprietor in full rig.

his audiences were often rowdy and troublesome, and Old John, hobbling into the ring with the aid of two sticks because he was lame in one leg, would brandish one of them at the audience and lecture them on their conduct. When he had finished everyone would jump to his feet shouting 'Bravo, Clarke!'

The son of the second John Clarke took over the show. He was referred to as a 'chip off the old block'. Another descendant of Old John, Alfred, became a great equestrian and married Annie Ginnett, one of another famous circus family. Their son, Alfred, sixth generation of circus performers, married the daughter of Phil Wirth of Australian circus fame, and Alfred's second son, John Frederick, another great equestrian, married Ida, Fred Ginnett's daughter. The second son of John Clarke the third, Charles, had his own circus: 'Clarke's Continental Circus'. His six children, three sons and three daughters, were all circus performers and fine riders. Charles had the ambition to make the finest aerial act in the world and he succeeded. For seven years 'The Clarkonians' practised and rehearsed before Charles thought they were ready to perform in public and when they did so they had an extraordinary and well-deserved success. Flying to the catch of Charles Clarke's hands, Ernie Clarke was the first to achieve the double somersault. The troupe joined Lord George Sanger's Circus in England and travelled with it all over the Continent. In 1901 the Clarkonians joined Barnum and Bailey's Circus, then in Paris, and went to America, where the family has since remained.

Ernie Clarke was also able to perform the triple somersault. It was said that he frequently gave private performances of a quadruple somersault to a catch, a feat so difficult as to seem incredible. It was never presented in public, as Ernie was never sure he could achieve it. He married Elizabeth Hannaford, of the famous Irish circus family, who, after performing in England, had gone to America in the early years of this century. The sixth generation of Clarkes is still performing in America.

Circus genealogy, both British and American, is bewildering, circus families intermarrying to such a degree that it is a problem to unravel the resulting complications. The Cookes, one of the earliest of the travelling circuses, intermarried with such circus families as Boswell (South Africa), Chadwick, Cole (America), Ginnett, Krember, (Germany), Lockhart, Macarte, Powell, Shelton, Wirth (Australia), Woolford, Austin, Clarke, Crockett, Cruickshank, Franks, Pinder, Rowland, Sanger, Transfeld and Yelding. As one goes on it becomes more and more chaotic. The Sangers married into the Pinder, Coleman, Austin, Hoffman, Freeman and Ginnett families; the Kayes with the Bakers, the Bakers with the Paulos, the Paulos with the Fossetts, the Fossetts with the Yeldings and the Yeldings with the Barretts. But these are the names which still fill the travelling English circuses.

By 1900 there were two hundred descendants of Thomas Cooke, the originator of the famous circus family. They were scattered all over the world, but most of them were circus artists. The Cookes claim as their ancestor Sir Thomas Cooke, Bart., of Holkham Hall, Norfolk. The first circus Cooke, Thomas, was born in Scotland in the middle of the eighteenth century and was a pioneer of the tenting show. Seldom moving south of the Tweed, he and his small company pitched on the outskirts of markets and fairs. In 1784, at Mauchlin, the poet Robert Burns was among the audience. In a boisterous mood that night the poet was so greatly taken with the playing of the one-man band, a fiddler, that he had him play one Scottish tune after another.

Thomas Cooke's son, Thomas Taplin Cooke, born at Warwick in 1782, was renowned for his feats of strength, leaping, horsemanship, and rope-walking, and so considerable were his earnings that he was able to buy a circus. He was the second of the English showmen to travel abroad (Astley having already established his Amphitheatre in Paris) and he and his company had a vogue at Lisbon in 1816. His was also the first circus to be involved in a storm at sea, for on the voyage home the ship was nearly wrecked in the Bay of Biscay and Thomas Taplin lost forty valuable horses. But with characteristic disdain of misfortune (a trait which remained with him throughout his life), as soon as he was safe on English soil he not only expended a large sum in the acquirement of a fresh stud of horses but also at great expense erected semi-permanent wooden amphitheatres at Newcastle-on-Tyne, Sunderland, Hull and other centres. Not content with this, in 1836 he ambitiously chartered the 'Royal Stuart' of Greenock to transport his entire company to New York. He had a hundred and thirty artists, forty of whom were members of the Cooke family and included his own seven sons and five daughters, a stud of forty-two horses and fourteen ponies, a circus band, servants and grooms. On the voyage a granddaughter was born and was named Oceana; she became a tight-rope

Opposite top Plates decorated with circus images designed by Laura Knight in 1934.

Opposite bottom *Big Top and Caravans* by E. Hesketh Hubbard

walker of international repute. In Paris she was the first to use a wire instead of a cord and it is recorded that 'when Oceana walked the slack wire the ring was invaded (by the smart set) until there was barely room enough for the wire to swing. If the box of resin was not there when her shoes needed treatment, there would be a race to fetch it for her'. But le Roux disapproved of her performances, saying she did not exert herself much but preferred to exhibit her beauty with reclining attitudes on the wire and by assuming voluptuous and indolent postures.

Disembarking at New York, Thomas Taplin built an amphitheatre of stone and brick in the Bowery. The success of his performances was extraordinary and night after night for six months he played to full houses and enthusiastic audiences. But once again a tale of success was interrupted by the old circus enemy – fire. The amphitheatre was burnt to the ground. Fortunately the horses had been stabled elsewhere and escaped disaster. Yet three weeks later Thomas Taplin opened a new circus at Philadelphia. Meanwhile another amphitheatre was in course of erection at Baltimore and when this was ready Thomas Taplin moved to it after a season of eight weeks at Philadelphia. Again there was a fire; this time everything, stud and properties, was completely destroyed. But Taplin was indomitable. Collecting a new stud of sixteen horses and with a smaller company, he performed for four months at Boston. Then, in 1837, he returned to Scotland, leaving behind in America his daughter Mary Ann, a noted horsewoman, 'The Amazon of the Sun', who had married William Cole, one of the circus staff. It is noteworthy that their son, William Washington Cole, became the founder of the famous American Cole Circus.

In England and Scotland Thomas Taplin once more resorted to building large wooden amphitheatres in which to give his performances. One of his playbills, dated 1842, was found in the hollow leg of an old table which a Dundee dealer was breaking up for scrap. Printed to advertise a benefit for 'Mr Cooke, Jnr. director of the arrangements and manager of the circle', it states that the performance was 'under the immediate patronage of Major Thorold and the officers of the 92nd Highlanders'. At the top of the bill was promised an act by Mr Cooke's daughter. 'For the first time in this town, she will make her appearance as the Goddess Minerva, and make a daring flight and ascension on a cable cord extended over the pit from the gallery to the ceiling of the circus. She will cast her personation after the style of Madame Saqui, the most celebrated rope-dancer of her day, and most popular of all the artists of Vauxhall, and will be seen in the midst of brilliant illumination and splendid glare of flame.' She also performed, according to the bills, 'a great feat of tight-rope balancing. Upon the narrow superfice of a tight-rope, she seats herself upon a chair, and before it is a table bearing a decanter, glasses and candles, and keeps her equilibrium with the greatest ease and self-possession.' On the same bill, incidentally, the clowns, at intervals, introduced 'their omnium gatherums of wit, American Saws and Joe Millerisms'.

In 1846, William Cooke, the second son of Thomas Taplin, was advertising his circus with a large and elaborate bill, with a space left for the date and place of performance to be written in. Printed in blue, red and black, it is ornamented with four large woodcuts, one representing the fight between Shaw, the life-guardsman, and a number of French soldiers at Waterloo, another showing the lady riders of the circus in a hunting scene, the third a beautiful horsewoman leaping through hoops of flowers, and the last a high-school rider in the flowing ring dress of the period. Mr Cooke announced 'the whole of his well-known colossal equestrian establishment of male and female artists of great celebrity and acknowledged talent; the stud of fifty highly trained horses and Lilliputian ponies; the leviathan entertainment of equestrian sports, hunting chases, tourney festivals, and battle scenes; the champion vaulters; the greatest clowns of the day; the smallest ponies in the world; and the trained Russian reindeer will all be exhibited to form the most extensive concentration of talent ever produced for one day's amusement. The elegant pavilion to be illuminated with portable gas.' The spectacle was to be the Battle of Waterloo, which followed the usual lines, opening with the French bivouac and closing with Wellington's victory. The ladies of the circus, mounted on cream Arab coursers, were to make an *entrée* and then came the circus proper. One suspects that the descendants of the old circus bill writers must, at some time, have joined the P.R. game; taking with them their adjectives but leaving much of their picturesqueness behind.

By the time Thomas Taplin Cooke died in 1866, most of his family of nineteen children had established themselves as circus performers, the third son, James Thorpe Cooke, being the most remarkable. Ducrow said: 'I have only seen *one* rider, and that is

Opposite A circus scene by Fernand Léger on a poster advertising an exhibition of his paintings, 1954.

A bandwagon from a touring circus arrives in Davenport, U.S.A.

James Cooke.'

A grandson of Thomas Taplin, John Henry, was born in New York during the season there in 1836. At the age of five he was an expert rope-walker and when he was eighteen he was known as 'the champion equestrian of the universe'. He travelled with Hengler, with Sanger, with Price in Portugal and Barnum in America. For two years he was principal artist and equestrian director of Franconi's circuses in Paris: the *Cirque d'Eté* and the *Cirque d'Hiver.* John Henry's daughter, Ernestine Rose, married Valdo the clown, a son of Chadwick; she, too, was an accomplished and graceful rider, and an unsigned article of the day captures the feeling of her act.

Whenever she appears she receives the heartiest of welcomes, the audience greeting her with bursts of enthusiasm, but this is not to be wondered at when one sees the excellence of her performances . . . . After the arena has been put in darkness, Miss Cooke appears, robed in black, upon a horse which is also draped in black. Limelight colours, being thrown upon her drapery, reveal her performing the unique feat of executing the elegant evolution of the Serpentine Dance while standing upon the back of her horse. Suddenly she leaves the horse, which now disappears, and she is seen flying round and round the building at a great height, clad in pure white robes resembling at one time an angel, the next a human butterfly. After a time she alights in the arena, where she finishes her performance with a pleasing dance in a most beautiful manner.

One of the Cookes' contracts is extant:

Cooke's Royal Circus,
Edinburgh   24 March, 1877.

Dear Sir,
        We the undersigned accept your services at terms stated: viz. £3 a week for a period of three months, with the option to re-engage you for another three months at the

expiration of the said three months' engagement. You are to perform to the best of your abilities and to abide by the rules and regulations of the establishments, to commence on Monday, 2 April, '77.

Respectfully yours,
The Bros. Cooke, Circus Proprietors

P.S. You must be here two or three days before your engagement commences, to practise, for which we are not liable in any way.

The proprietors of the circus were then the brothers John Henry and Harry Welby Cooke and their cousin, Alfred Eugene Cooke. Leon Douglas Cooke, son of John Henry and husband of Iona Ginnett, a great rider, is still acting as a ringmaster.

One of the finest family circuses in England is that of the Rosaires. This circus was founded by Freddy Ross, who was born in 1877 at Saddlesworth, a small village on the borders of Yorkshire and Lancashire. His courtesy title in the circus world was Count Rosaire. His mother derived from circus performers, his father worked on the fairgrounds, his uncle, Billy Ross, the nine-stone-four-pound champion of England, once vanquished Frank Craig, the Coffee Cooler. The Count himself was something of a pugilist. When he was fifteen, the family then living at Oldham, he and his two older brothers practised at the local gymnasium where they got a grounding in circus acrobatics. One of his earliest feats was to jump on a scythe blade in his bare feet and cut two potatoes in half as he did so. The three brothers formed an act, known as the Ross Combination, and obtained a week's engagement at the Gaiety Theatre, Oldham, at a salary of £4 per week. Halfway through the week they were offered and accepted a six months' engagement at £6. Then his mother financed a small booth show for the boys, who performed on the fairgrounds, but this did not last long. Separating from his brothers, the Count met with many vicissitudes, for a time becoming a contortionist and jumper with Harrison on a 'square show'. He walked from Allerton to Lancaster as Harrison declared he had no money for his fare. He arrived deadbeat, hungry, without a penny in his pocket and with toothache. Harrison refused an advance, so he and the Count parted company, the Count sleeping that night under the tiltings of a roundabout. He met a Negro and busked with him for a week, doing stilt-walking, clowning and acrobatics, then he got a job with Sedgewick's Menagerie which featured the Great Lorenzo, a lion tamer of the old 'hustling' school. The Count's role was to amuse the

American citizens line the streets to watch the Forepaugh and Sells elephants go by.

crowd while the cage was being built for the lions. Once Billington, the public hangman, was among the audience. 'I put in one or two tricks with the rope that night to show him he wasn't the only man who could handle one,' the Count drily remarked on one occasion. He was soon out of a job again, once more stilt-walking in the streets and going round with a cap. But he never forgot for a moment his ambition to be a circus performer and one day have his own circus, and when he came across a small circus and begged the proprietor to take him on, he was heartbroken and bewildered to be told that he was not good enough to be employed.

In a Staffordshire town, a girl standing at the door of a hotel smiled at his clown's

Right Camels lead the Ringlings' parade through an American town at the turn of the century.

Above Barnum's circus parade on Pennsylvania Avenue, Washington DC.

costume and his face smeared with a white make-up. The Count jumped from his stilts, dangled the cap in front of her and asked for a kiss. 'What,' she said 'with a face like that?' That was his first meeting with the Countess. Her father owned half a dozen hotels and some small music-halls; the old 'free and easies'. The Countess was managing one of the hotels. 'A handsome girl she was,' the Count would say reminiscently. The next evening he was in the hotel and she gave him something for his toothache. 'It cured it,' the Count said. A month later they were married and working together on music-halls, the Count whistling, the Countess playing the piano. But it did not satisfy one whose ambition was still the circus. The chance came at Beswick. A showman with a strong-man act had a bitter quarrel with his wife, and in his rage was about to break up

The Ringling Brothers' clowns on top of a bandwagon in a parade in 1919.

Top A wild-animal wagon built for Barnum, Bailey and Hutchinson in the early 1880s.

Centre The Beauty Tableau, adorned with six carved wooden female figures, was originally built in the late 1890s.

Centre The Lion and Mirror bandwagon. The Adam Forepaugh circus ordered this magnificent wagon to be built in 1879 with a telescoping tableau on top for parades. In 1890 it was acquired by Ringling Brothers for use in their first railroad circus.

Right The huge Asia Tableau, originally built in 1903 for the Barnum and Bailey circus, could accommodate a band on the top.

his 'square' show. 'Don't do that,' the Count said. 'I'll give you £4 for it, cash down, on the spot.' The strong man disgustedly told him to take it away. At Ripponden, the owner of a roundabout lent him some tiltings. This was the beginning of Rosaire's Circus. The Countess made her own dresses and Fred's costumes, and pattered on the 'walk up'. In tights, moustache carefully waxed, Fred postured on the platform and gave a promise of his prowess and when the booth was tolerably full he disappeared inside and gave his one-man show. Performances did not last long, then back to the 'walk up' to cajole another audience inside.

It was a strenuous life. When the fairground emptied of the crowd and the naphtha flares began to flicker, the booth was dismantled, packed on a handcart and trundled to the next pitch. The weather was biting cold and often the moisture on the Countess's face froze as she stood outside the show and pattered to get the people in. The first night the takings were £12. It was not always like this. When business was bad, and often it was, the Count would offer to fight any man of his own weight for £1. He was never beaten. On the fairground at Ripponden, to the beatings of the showman's drums and the music of the hurdy-gurdies, the Rosaire's first child, Aubrey, destined to be one of the great clowns of the tenting circus, was born. He was the 'Jimmie Green' of tradition and was adored and beloved of children. He died in 1939.

During the autumn of their first 'square show' the Count bought the top of a round tent from Ted Hodgini for £15, and all through the winter the Countess stitched canvas to make wallings so that during the following spring Rosaire's Circus, 'the one-man circus', took the road. It continued for five or six years, a time of incredible struggles and rapidly growing family. But slowly a good show was being built up, the Count more and more confident that he was well on the way to being the owner of a big circus. Then came the calamity of the First World War. All but one of the horses were commandeered, the show had to be broken up. The living-wagon was pitched in a field at South Harley.

The 'France' bandwagon was built in 1918. It is the only vehicle left of a series of fifteen, each depicting a different country.

Savings dwindled, for there were already five children to keep and Vivienne was on the way. The living-wagon had to be sold and Fred made a new one. After unbelievable makeshifts, the family somehow surviving, Fred got a job as a coal miner. But when peace came he started all over again. He built a 'square show' and after a season he bought a roundabout top which served as the nucleus for a one-pole tent.

In 1926 the Count joined forces with Barrett, and 'Barrett's Amalgamated Circus' with its large tent toured the south-west. It was a failure. There was a blow-down; the Count and Barrett parted company but the Count retained the tent. With that tent he climbed to success. It was the real beginning of the Rosaire Circus as a family show. Vivienne, Cissie and Fred performed on the trapeze, Dennis on the wire, Derrick helped him,

Aubrey and Ivor on the rings, Zena did a contortionist act, Vivienne a riding act. Fred and Aubrey clowned and the Countess was the 'equestrian director'.

Before the Second World War the Count was able to introduce elephants into the ring, later a cage of lions, trained by Martin Hawkes, the son of a clergyman. Hawkes, intended for the Church, had, after his university days, decided on the circus; his real interest in life was animals. He married Ida Rosaire at Sevenoaks, his father officiating at the marriage ceremony in his own church.

The Count died at the circus's winter quarters at Billericay on 9 November 1949, at the age of seventy-two. A man of great courage, firm as a rock, with intense but quiet feelings, he was kind and generous and always loyal to his friends. He hardly ever spoke in temper, never unkindly, never grumbled and had a quiet sense of humour. He had great hopes, wild impulses and a sanguine temperament. Like many of the circus folk, he had a love of natural beauty, seldom expressed. He was happiest in the early morning when, with a charming smile lighting his face, he would start on the morning ride to the next tober, sitting in that queer contraption of his which he called a trap, and driving the horses. He gloried in the freshness of the early morning, the green of the country, the singing of the birds. From the humblest beginnings he succeeded in establishing one of the finest tenting circuses in England and he trained his children to become circus artists of the highest rank. All his family were noted for their beauty.

The story of Madame Clara Paulo and her circus is also one of tremendous courage, of incredible vicissitudes, and of an unquenchable spirit which eventually triumphed over all difficulties. Like the Rosaires, the family was eight in number: six girls, Emily, Lizzie, Madge, Grace, Evelyn, Clara; and two boys, Harry and Frank. All were married, mostly to other circus performers. Madame Paulo was one of the few women who have owned circuses in England. She also showed the horses in the ring and walked the wire. Her forebears were in the show business for generations. Her father, William Wilson,

Right The Hagenbeck-Wallace Circus Annex, a collection of 'human oddities', operating in Brooklyn in 1931.

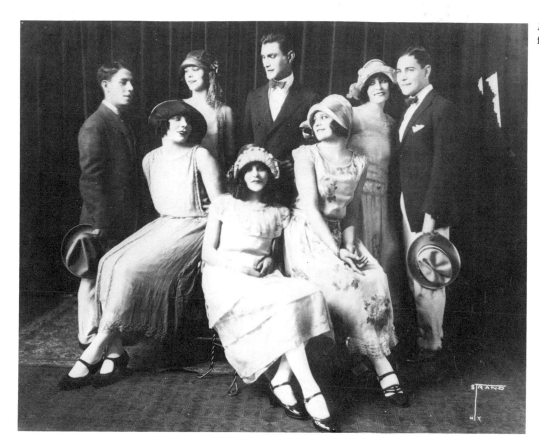

Left The Colleano family, one of the most famous names in circus history.

The excitement is over and the circus settles
down for the night.

This photograph of a circus in Paris in the late nineteenth century shows a stand of performing dogs and a 'monkey palace'.

was well known on the fairgrounds; her mother, Elizabeth Silvester, was a clown and a jester. Her brothers were acrobats, posturers and benders. Her husband was Frank Paulo, whose mother, Madame Blondin, walked a rope over Niagara Falls, but was not so successful when she essayed to walk a rope stretched from one church steeple to another in Bolton. She was about to start when the rope broke and had to be knotted. When she was halfway across the knot turned, she stumbled and as she fell clutched the rope with her hands. There she clung until a blanket was fetched and stretched beneath her; into this she dropped, but was badly hurt.

Madame Paulo's father and mother had a small circus; while they were travelling in Scotland her mother went into labour, their wagon was pulled into a yard in Edinburgh and here Madame Paulo was born. She went into the ring when she was three years old, 'trying to perform some little trick; we all had our hardships, no money, no food, my mother had a hard struggle to bring us all (a family of fourteen) up healthy.' Madame Paulo was eighteen when Frank Paulo came to work on her father's circus and they were soon married.

The young pair joined Buff Bill's (William Kayes) Menagerie; Clara walked the wire, Frank showed a fortune-telling pony. With this show they went to Ireland, and here,

after further experience with Ned Hannaford's circus, Frank decided to start on his own. The beginning was modest – songs and dances were performed on the flap of a wagon and Clara walked the wire. The takings depended on the sale of tickets for prizes. They opened at a small village in the south of Ireland, on the first day the prizes cost six shillings and they sold three shillings' worth of tickets. Performances were given at crossroads and soon they were able to add a hoop-la and a gun stall to their attractions, while on Sunday donkey and pony races were staged. The life was precarious, but there was just enough to live on and somehow Frank contrived to buy a small tent. The southern Irish hated the English and although usually they had a soft heart for the circus folk, after one performance bricks were thrown at the tent and at Cork a gang broke in and wrecked everything. The tent was beyond repair, it had to be abandoned and the old life of performing at crossroads resumed. Frank 'spieled' from the caravan steps; at the rear a rough ring was marked on the turf and after every act the hat was passed round. Often performances were started with the family hungry and when a few coppers were in the hat Lizzie would be sent running for bread and cheese. Clara was born and on the following day Madame, with the child strapped to her, kissed the Blarney Stone at Killarney and wished that her child should never join a circus.

Top A European circus family enjoying a meal in their caravan.

Left A muscular group of circus performers in Marseilles at the beginning of the century

At the outbreak of the First World War they hurried back to England and Frank enlisted and went to France, leaving the living-wagon pitched on Home Moor. Frank's allowance was insufficient to feed the family so that, in the winter, wood was chopped and sold from door to door while young Frank collected coppers in the streets with his acrobatics. In 1917 his father, back from the war, spent part of his gratuity on a couple of horses which he broke for the ring, and Clara was taught to ride. Old Frank managed to buy a tent cheaply, and acquired another six horses and an old lion. The wagon was painted yellow and black and once more the Paulo Circus took the road. For years the show did moderately well, though never well enough for the family to rest in the winter. At Wombwell, at the end of the winter in 1928, Anderton and Rowland, then in Cornwall, proposed that the two shows should amalgamate. A contract was signed and the Paulo Circus started on a three hundred and fifty miles journey to St Austell with fourteen loads and seventy-five horses. When the circus reached Rotherham, Old Frank, who had never had a day's illness in his life, suddenly collapsed with pneumonia and had to be taken to hospital. 'Keep going,' he said to Madame Clara, 'don't wait for me.' The next day she rode a horse bareback away from the travelling show back to the hospital. When she reached the show again she was asked how he was. 'Dying,' she replied. That night her sister went back in a car for news. It was not until the show was within fifty miles of St Austell that she returned. To Clara she said: 'I know you'll have to cry. But it won't make no matter. He's dead.'

It was a bad summer. The next winter was worse, for there were storms and snow and the circus had to rest in Plymouth. But Madame took it out again in January, for with all her money gone she had to go on to live. It was another lean season and that winter Madame was forced to sell everything. She did not get much for the tent and six horses went for £100 and the other horses were sold in twos and threes. Madge went to Sir Robert Fossett's circus, where Bob gave her a horse to ride; Grace went to Proctor's and danced and performed on the wire. For the next three years the family was scattered, working at different circuses. Madame scraped and saved and somehow they got another show together.

Just before the Second World War her fortunes changed, for the show had become too good not to attract and was thronged at every performance. Prosperity continued throughout the war when the little family circus came into its own. Paulo's became one of the most prosperous tenting shows in the country, with Frank Foster as manager and ringmaster.

So, when the Second World War was finished, two grand old ladies of the circus vied with each other, quite unmaliciously, to see which could outlive the other. The

Above left Practising acrobatic tricks before the show.

Above right Itinerant artists enjoy a joke outside their caravan in the Sussex countryside.

Countess Rosaire won, but now both of them, if one may be permitted a sentimental obituary, have gone to their winter quarters.

These accounts of tenting circuses show how difficult the first two decades of this century were for circus performers. Astley's had been demolished for over a decade, and Hengler's, in Argyll Street, the last of the permanent circus buildings (of which, at one time, there had been so many), had been transformed into the Palladium music-hall, while in Oxford Street, a bare hundred yards from the scene of Hengler's aquatic triumphs and from where his daughter, Jenny Louise, had entranced Londoners with her horsemanship, a bizarre contraption called the bioscope, a sort of glorified penny-plain magic lantern, had thrown jerky pictures on a screen, continuous photographs taken from the box of a puffing railway engine. (Often the smoke from the engine obscured the pictures.) On the fairgrounds, booths were devoted to these moving pictures and showed shorts of hectic life in the Wild West with an accompaniment of revolver shots, cracking whips and the music of a calliope; an incredible hotchpotch of melodrama. But the music-hall was now the popular entertainment and those of the circus folk whose acts could be adapted to the halls had already abandoned the tenting show – the acrobats, the contortionists, the jugglers, the trapeze artists, the wire-walkers and trick-cyclists were earning music-hall salaries which the circus could no longer afford. Even the clowns went to become red-nosed comedians. Others who could not bring themselves to break with the circus migrated abroad, some to the German, French and Italian circuses, others to America. It was said of this time that one had only to stand outside any Continental circus and shout 'Bill' or 'Joe' and an Englishman would appear.

Only fresh ideas and a great showman with determination to restore the circus to its old popularity could save the situation. The man appeared. But he was faced with a grim task.

The new Olympia structure at West Kensington had been opened as far back as 1885. The Paris Hippodrome Circus gave a season there in 1886-7, and two years later Barnum's appeared, while in 1900-1 Barnum and Bailey's Circus came, followed by Sir Charles Cochran in 1906 and 1913, when he presented Hagenbeck's Zoo and one of the finest circuses seen in London. Then, in 1919, Wilkins and Young staged a circus there. It was a good circus but suffered by comparison with the excellence of Cochran's show.

During the First World War Bertram Mills had been a Captain in the R.A.S.C., buying fodder for Army horses. He was now back in civilian life, uncertain as to what his future activities were to be, for his coach-building premises had been commandeered and there

Above left A French circus band waiting for the show to begin.

Top The thrilling moment when the posters are pasted up. Chipperfield's Circus comes to town in 1946.

Above Jimmy Chipperfield looks on as the crew hoist the Big Top.

111

was a slump in the carriage-building trade. He was invited by friends to share a box at Olympia and see the circus, and after the performance he was asked what he thought of it. In effect he said if he couldn't put on a better show he'd eat his hat and that notwithstanding the fact that he hardly knew an English performer by sight. Amid the laughter Lord Daresbury bet him £100 that he would not.

Mills was now forty-seven, his technical knowledge of the circus was small, although he had always had a great love for horses and had learnt to ride when he was three. He had left school at the age of fifteen and passed into his father's coach-building works at Paddington, his first job being to wash down the coaches. At the age of eighteen he went to the States, travelling steerage and landing with a capital of £20. Returning to

England, he was the first to build an American show wagon, and this, now known as the Mills Wagon, is still used at horse shows for single and pair harness horses. He frequently travelled to the Continent to exhibit coaches and horses at such places as the *Concours Hippique* in Paris and similar shows at Brussels, The Hague, and many other towns. At these horse shows there was often a circus, and Mills, with little to do in the morning, got into the habit of strolling into the circus tent and watching the rehearsals and practice, particularly the training and schooling of the circus animals. Occasionally he sat and watched a circus in England and felt that what was lacking in the entertainment was not its appeal but the fact that it was out of touch with the times.

And now he was faced with the task of putting on a circus better than the one he had seen. At first it seemed that he would succeed without much difficulty, for in the early part of 1920 John Ringling's friend, the late John McEntee, of the Bowman Biltmore Hotels, was in London and promised Mills to approach Ringling on his return to America. The result of this was that Ringling agreed to bring the famous American circus of Ringling, Barnum and Bailey to Olympia for the season of 1920-1, and Mills went forward with his arrangements. In July Ringling cabled that he could not fulfil his promise, for he had found the difficulties of transporting his circus across the Atlantic to be insurmountable. But, said Ringling, if Mills could, by hook or crook, get a show together on his own, then, win or lose, Ringling would stand by him. Mills described it as the most sporting offer he had ever received in his life and as it happened he was already so deeply involved financially that all he could do was to go on, which he did. He began to plan a programme, believing that his only real chance of success was to assemble at Olympia the finest talent of America, the Continent and what there was of England. One handicap was that ex-enemy artists were still barred from performing in England by a Ministry of Labour regulation, and this stopped consideration of many renowned German and Austrian horse, trapeze and acrobatic acts. Mills had already been to the Continent and visited many circuses there; now he went to America. On his homeward

Above A chain of men establish the quarter poles for Bertram Mills touring circus.

Opposite Four styles of circus poster from the USSR, Germany and Switzerland.

journey he was able to pencil a skeleton programme.

He engaged people for his executive and staff and in his anxiety to be uninfluenced by other people's conceptions of how he should run his circus he would have nobody who had been in the circus business before. He now had a clear conception of what he wanted and surrounded himself with men who could understand his ideas and carry them out, irrespective of what tradition had to say about them.

The preparation of that first circus gave Mills the most trying and anxious weeks of his life. Not only was a tremendous amount of money at stake but also his future success as a showman. He surmounted one difficulty after another, for as soon as one had been solved another presented itself. The seating for six thousand people, the acoustics, the exactly right position for the bandstand, the smooth working of the acts in the ring, the *tempo* of the performance as a whole, all these were problems. The climax came with the dress rehearsal. Instead of the calculated two and a half hours, it dragged on for four. Mills began to wonder whether he would have the show ready for the next and opening day. He sat through the night with the ringmaster, deleting, cutting acts to ribbons and speeding up. At eight o'clock the next morning he was back in the ring for another rehearsal. That afternoon, with no outward appearance of the strain through which he had gone, Mills stood at the ring entrance and watched his first parade march across the ring. His nerves were strung to the utmost. But success was assured from the first performance.

'When I launched my first circus at Olympia,' Mills was to write in the programme of his tenth season, 'it was "drawing a bow at a venture". I had had no experience of the entertainment world, but, as a boy, I loved a circus. In 1920 I was looking for a job; the carriage and harness business, in which I was fully employed before the War, had practically come to a standstill. I felt the need of a big circus . . . . and perhaps, also, of a permanent one in London. Finding that Olympia was free for the following Christmas, I leased it for a period of seven weeks. The first circus was a success beyond all my hopes. I had expected to sink a considerable amount of money which might be spread over a number of years, but in practically "drawing even" the first year I was more than agreeably surprised.'

In appearance, Mills, with his ruddy complexion, his twinkling eyes and rather stocky figure, suggested the typical English sporting horseman. Always well dressed, a cornflower in his buttonhole, more often than not a cigar in his mouth, he had a Dickensian air which went well with his character as a showman. It was solely owing to his courage, his flair for organisation, his appreciation of what was finest in the circus, and his imagination, that the circus in England was again taken to the hearts of the public. It was the work which he did at Olympia and with his tenting circus which was the immediate cause of the immense popularity of the circus during recent years and more particularly the years of the Second World War, and it must be remembered that there are now as many as forty to fifty circuses on the road during the tenting season. Mills was the first in England to recognise that the *tempo* of the one-ring circus performance must be accelerated. He said that the interest of the public 'must never be allowed to flag, the so-called comic *entrées* must be cut and "padding" in every class of act must be ruthlessly eliminated.' Only those who know the fierce pride of circus artists in their acts and work will appreciate the struggles Mills must have had with them to get what he wanted. He always saw his programme as a whole and not in terms of acts, so he sacrificed everything to the programme.

Despite the handicap of repeated illness, he achieved his outstanding success by grim determination. First he had to acquire that technical knowledge which would have been second nature had he come of a circus family, and he was well aware of this necessity and his attitude towards his artists was almost one of diffidence. He once said that he was an 'amateur' directing the work of professionals. Many of his dealings were with Continental artists and he spoke no language but his own, yet he always seemed to attain his requirements.

Mills made his circus at Olympia the goal of all circus artists, whatever their nationality. To appear in it was either to crown a reputation or to make one. Year after year Mills engaged the most outstanding acts in the world and for circus-lovers this gave his programme a unique excitement, for he gave them the opportunity of seeing all those performers who indeed excelled.

The 'Guv'nor', for as such he was widely known, had endless energy and a tremendous capacity for work. His normal working hours were anything from sixteen

Opposite Behind the scenes, hours of intricate work go into making the brilliant costumes for circus artistes.

Above Bertram Mills, the great English circus proprietor, who started up in response to a bet.

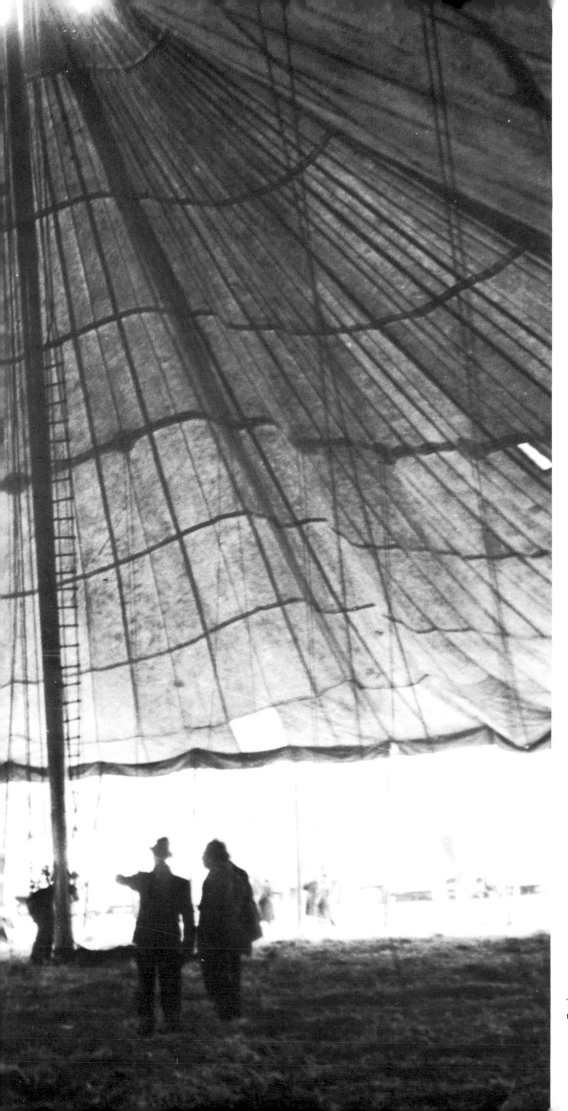

The Big Top and the King Pole are
up ready for Bertram Mills Circus.

Full dress rehearsal. Liberty horses perform their solo at Bertram Mills' Circus, Olympia.

to eighteen hours a day. On one occasion a friend went to Southampton to say goodbye to Mills who was going to America on the 'Queen Mary', due to depart the following morning. He found Mills in his cabin with a pile of two thousand letters before him, which were to be sent off on behalf of a charity ball of which Mills was the chairman. Although it was already late in the evening, Mills insisted that each one of these should have his personal signature and he had already been signing them for an hour. He worked until six-thirty next morning, when, the last having been finished, he went off to the ship's kitchen in search of coffee and sandwiches. When, at Bournemouth, his tent was torn to shreds by a fierce gale he was at his home at Chalfont St Giles. It was midnight on a Saturday evening when a voice on the telephone informed him of the disaster, but Mills at once motored to Ascot, the winter quarters of his circus, where there was a reserve tent. Before the circus train drew in at Bognor on the Sunday morning, Mills was already on the tober with the reserve tent waiting for the arrival of the tentmaster. He had accompanied the lorries which had driven through the night with the tent and necessary gear.

It was also late at night when news reached him that three tigers had escaped just as Togare was about to show them to an audience at Devonport. This, he felt, demanded his personal investigation, and as the last train from Paddington to Plymouth had already gone, Mills got into his car and raced to Reading, where he clambered on to a milk train. He was on the tober at five in the morning when the only person awake on the ground was the night watchman.

His greatest passions in life were horses and coaching. When he was sixteen he frequently travelled on the driver's box of the London to Oxford coach, even sometimes holding the reins. Before breakfast he persuaded the drivers of the old horse-buses plying between Paddington and the Elephant and Castle to let him handle the reins. When he got back to Paddington he started his day's work. Tom Tagg, who drove the last night coach from London to Brighton, taught him to drive a team. In 1936 he acted as coachman to 'Mr Pickwick' when he and other immortals from the pages of *The Pickwick Papers* travelled by coach from Charing Cross to Rochester. Wearing his grey top-hat, he was invariably at meetings of the Coaching Club in Hyde Park and he drove at the Richmond Horse Show. In the entrance hall of his home in the Chilterns were racks of hunting-crops and coaching-whips, while near the lodge gates the stables were full, not of circus horses but of hacks and hunters. He used to declare that driving a team of horses did him more good than any medicine. A year or two before his death he had been seriously ill with influenza. Disobeying his doctors, he got out of his bed one morning and motored to Olympia, where his favourite team of blacks, harnessed to his coach, waited his coming. That afternoon he drove them to Ranelagh and next day he won the Marathon competition with them.

Mills had a great knowledge of horses. Like Astley, he thought there was only one way to train them, and that was with patience and carrots. His liberty horses were specially bred for him in Hungary and trained at Ascot, and were among the finest horses that have ever been shown in a circus ring, while his pad horses were of an equally high standard. He could never resist buying horses and coaches and when he died he possessed eighteen coaches, all beautiful examples of design and craftsmanship, which were sold off later.

Above all he was a showman. The pageantry and pomp which marked the opening each year of his circus at Olympia could only have been planned and carried out by a great showman. The Lord Mayor of London on his arrival at the circus was greeted by flowers handed to him by the assembled artists in their circus costumes. This was followed by a lunch for fourteen hundred guests, who included Royalty, the Lord Mayor, diplomats, Cabinet Ministers, stars and sportsmen. At the performance, Lord Lonsdale would step into the ring and present the performers with bouquets.

It is, perhaps, in keeping with the character of Bertram Mills that as a boy he played in a Salvation Army band, though the instrument was not a big drum. In a mission-hall off the Edgware Road he met General Evangeline Booth, and forty years later, when Mills was with his tenting show at Torquay, they met again. The General remarked: 'As a boy you played the cornet in the first corps of which I had the command – when my father made me a Lieutenant. I have had three commissioners from that corps and I am sorry that you did not stay in the Army.'

Mills died on 16 April 1938, at the age of sixty-five, the day on which his tenting show opened for the season. Gustave Fréjaville, a great authority on the circus, in an obituary notice in the *Petit Parisien* wrote: '*Bertram Mills, roi du cirque, parfait spécialiste du cheval, était un gentleman correct et affable; il savait se montrer l'hôte le plus courtois et le plus attentif – ses deux fils pareillement et particulièrement sympathiques possèdent toute l'autorité et compétence nécessaire pour continuer dignement son oeuvre.*'

Fréjaville was right. The show went on for another twenty years under the able administration of the two sons, Bernard and Cyril until, it may be thought, Bertram Mills's Circus became in this unhappy age, an anachronism.

Invitation to the tenting circus.

5

Acts and Accidents

We hear of rope-walkers as far back as Roman times and the modern wire-walker is little more than an improvement on the ancient and medieval rope-walkers who entertained our early forefathers.

The first of the greatest was Madame Saqui, who appeared in Vauxhall Gardens in 1816. She mounted the rope at midnight in a dress glittering with tinsel and spangles, her head surmounted by a great plume of ostrich feathers. There was a brilliant display of fireworks, the sparks flying around her as she danced on the rope above thousands of spectators. Then thirty-two years old, the masculine formation of her face and her enormous muscles gave her the appearance of an under-sized man. Marguerite Lalanne, for that was her real name, had an extraordinary career of wealth and penury. The daughter of Jean-Baptiste Lalanne, she was taught at an early age the rudimentary technique of rope-walking in the company of La Malaga, her future rival. The two little girls worked hard to perfect themselves in the various tricks such as the timing of the rope, the making of the turn and the cross steps. But they were not yet allowed to attempt the perilous leap through a hoop of fire, the triumph of Navarin the Famous, with Nicolet and Forioso at the Tivoli Gardens. Saqui's real career began at the time of the Revolution; her days under Napoleon were glorious and it was with his permission that she followed the bivouacs of the Imperial Guard. During the Restoration she was fêted and continued to live splendidly, but with the flamboyant years of Louis-Philippe her fortunes declined and she ended miserably and lamentably, performing in the tawdry and obscure hippodromes of the Second Empire until the day of her death in 1866. When she was seventy-one her poverty was such that she was still compelled to dance on the rope to satisfy her modest wants. In those last years she could be seen, a mummified old woman, entirely dressed in black, furtively gliding along *l'avenue de Neuilly* to her squalid lodging. After her death, in the drawer of a desk was found a heap of pawn-tickets, for the poor old lady at the last had been compelled to pledge all she had, the modest pieces of jewellery and all the other treasured souvenirs of her strange life. She was remembered only by an old Italian woman, who lived to be a centenarian, and who, until she died, had Masses said for the repose of Saqui's soul and believed that, in order to expiate her pride, Madame Saqui was condemned to wander for two hundred years between earth and sky, her only amusement to walk and dance on a rainbow's edge.

A German successor of the early nineteenth century was Wilhelm Kolter, the son of a celebrated bareback-rider. There is a pleasing legend of his encounter with Jack Barred, the English rope-walker, at the Congress of Monarchs at Aix-la-Chapelle in 1818. Jack

Barred had stretched a rope from the top windows of tall houses across a street, performing on it to the edification of the assembled monarchs and their retinues. Hardenberg, the Prussian minister, watching him, thought of Kolter, whom he had seen in Berlin, and sent for him. When one morning Barred stepped on to the rope he was astonished to see a man dressed as a merchant but without a balancing pole advancing towards him from the other end. The two men met in the centre, neither would give way, until Kolter, with a tremendous leap, jumped over Barred's head, regained the rope with his feet, and laughingly danced his way to the window.

A greater figure in the history of rope-walking is that of the immortal Jean François Gravelet, known as Blondin. The son of one of Napoleon's officers, he was born in 1824.

Below L'Estrange, one of Blondin's many imitators who was known as the 'Australian Blondin' crossing the Middle Harbour at Port Jackson.

Below The celebrated Blondin who could play the violin, somersault and cook omelettes whilst balancing on the tight-rope.

Bottom Blondin made his name by walking along a rope suspended above Niagara Falls. He was enthusiastically received at the Crystal Palace in 1861 where he was paid £1,200 for twelve performances.

CRYSTAL PALACE.

SATURDAY, 1 JUNE, 1861.

BLONDIN

OR

NIAGARA CELEBRITY

WILL MAKE HIS

FIRST ASCENT IN ENGLAND

IN THE UPPER PORTION OF THE GREAT TRANSEPT, ON

Saturday, 1st June, 1861, at Four o'Clock precisely.

ADMISSION, – HALF-A-CROWN,

OR BY

SEASON TICKET.

RESERVED STALLS HALF-A-CROWN EXTRA.

The Doors of the Palace will be opened at Ten o'Clock.

Frequent Trains will run throughout the **Day**, but to prevent disappointment visitors by Rail are earnestly recommended to avail themselves of Trains early in the Day.

When he was six he was so excited by the performance of some travelling acrobats that his father placed him in the *Ecole de Gymnase* at Lyons. Here he made his first public appearance as an equilibrist and was called 'The Little Wonder'. The Ravel family of acrobats offered him an engagement which he accepted and so travelled with them to America. At the age of thirty-five he crossed Niagara Falls on a rope hung a hundred and sixty feet above the basin of the falls. Halfway across he lay on the rope at full length and turned a backward somersault. He landed amid scenes of tremendous enthusiasm, a band playing the *Marseillaise*. Then he made the return journey carrying a chair; this he balanced on two legs on the rope and sat on it. Then he stood on the chair on one leg. He repeated the performance in July and August of the same year, crossing this time blindfolded and with a man on his back. On one occasion he crossed in the character of a Siberian slave and stood on his head on the rope. In 1860 he rope-walked across the falls on stilts. Albert Edward, the Prince of Wales, was present amongst the spectators, so Blondin suggested that the Prince should accompany him. His Royal Highness declined, saying that his rank obliged him to stay where he was. This reply of the Prince was one of Blondin's favourite jokes.

In 1862 Blondin appeared at the Crystal Palace, receiving a fee of £1,200 for twelve performances. Now he enacted a chef and cooked himself an omelette on the rope. He also played the March from *William Tell* on a violin, and danced and somersaulted at the same time. The Governors of the Crystal Palace, having netted a profit of £10,000, gratefully presented him with a gold medal. At Sheffield he wheeled a lion cub in a barrow across the rope. He died in his villa home at Northfields, Ealing, in 1898 at the age of seventy-five, and although his house has long since been demolished the new thoroughfare which crosses its site has been named Niagara Avenue.

Blondin had many imitators, among them several would-be female Blondins. One of these was Mrs Powell, who appeared at a fête in Aston Park, Birmingham, in July 1863. She was thirty-six years of age and had been walking the tight-rope for thirty-three of them, but on this occasion her long experience failed her. A sack was placed over her head, for she was to walk the rope blindfolded, but she had hardly gone a yard when she slipped and fell to her death.

Of recent times perhaps the most distinguished name is that of Con Colleano. Described as 'The Wizard of the Tight Wire', he brought a new excitement and aesthetic satisfaction into the circus. Picturesquely dressed as a matador, he advanced into the ring and with his scarlet *capo* made the traditional passes at a bull. So vivid was the mental image he evoked that the audience saw not a circus ring but the sun-drenched arena of a Spanish town, the ritual and the pageant of an actual bull-fight. Then he mounted the wire and performed *tangos, jotas* and *fandangos* with the unsurpassed grace of a *prima ballerina*. A dance was interrupted with a somersault, and while he actually made the curve in the air of this, he stripped off his loose silk trousers and regained the wire in silver knee-breeches. His final trick was the amazing one of a forward somersault, feet to feet, and, as truly announced by the ringmaster, 'the only artist in the world to accomplish it'.

One must not forget the jugglers, especially Cinquevalli and Rastelli, who were the most accomplished of them all, but while Cinquevalli was a finished performer and a good showman he was not the equal of Rastelli. Cinquevalli was born at Lissa, then a part of Prussia, in 1859. His real name was probably Emile Otto Braun, although this has been given variously as Lehmann and Kestner. Educated in Berlin, he started as an acrobat and a wire-walker, while as a boy he also worked on the trapeze and was billed as 'The Little Flying Devil'. One of his early feats was to walk a high rope stretched over the River Bugg, but a bad fall from the trapeze resulted in hospital for several weeks and since juggling had always attracted him he devoted his idleness to practice, concentrating on the use of a few props.

He came to London in 1885 to appear at a Christmas circus at Covent Garden. He was number eight on the programme and was described as *Signor Paul Cinquevalli. L'Incomparable. Exercises Extraordinaires. Les Jeux Amusants*. He had always been fascinated by the movement of billiard balls and this had prompted him to learn several of his more intricate tricks.

He had great courage and fortitude. Once, at the Newcastle-on-Tyne Empire, the plate he held to catch the balls in the air broke in fragments and cut his fingers to the bone, while a ball dropped on to his foot and smashed his toes. Suffering intense pain, he completed his act. Then appearances were interrupted by the First World War, when it

was remembered that he was a German by birth and he was boycotted. This broke his heart and probably shortened his life. He died in 1918.

If ever an artist worked to achieve perfection it was Rastelli. He was never satisfied with himself. In the ring, dressed in a white costume, suit, belt, knickerbockers, stockings and shoes, he performed his amazing juggling feats with a modesty of manner and a complete absence of showmanship which made the public underestimate his technique, but the ease with which he worked had taken years of ceaseless practice to acquire. He was the son of an Italian circus family and was born on his father's tenting show. His father wished to train him to take his place as director and tried to suppress the boy's ambition to be a juggler. But he practised secretly, notwithstanding the many beatings he received when his father caught him. 'You'll never make money that way,' was the invariable reprimand. 'Anyone can juggle if they practise long enough.' Long enough! If only life was long enough for all the practice that was necessary, the practice that would enable him to achieve something beyond the triumphs of all jugglers before him. He continued to practise, until finally he was allowed to juggle openly, appearing as a juggler in the family ring. Henry Sherek saw him at Naples and offered him a contract to appear at the Paris Alhambra followed by an English tour; Rastelli accepted.

Rastelli married a tight-rope walker of the celebrated Price family. He went from success to success. He appeared at Olympia and on one American tour he made a fortune. The finale of his act was spectacular in the extreme and always aroused the audience to a fever of enthusiasm, for he juggled with three flaming torches which he threw so high that it seemed they would reach the circus top. He died in 1932 as the

Above left A spectacular performance by Daniso Martini, the Italian slack-rope walker and juggler.

Above right Inspired by Blondin's feat, Signorina Maria Spelterina crosses the rapids of Niagara Falls, 1867.

result of a stupid accident – blood-poisoning following a wound in the mouth.

But perhaps more characteristic of the circus are the equestrians and equestriennes, who may also be said to go back to Roman times in some of their skills and practices. We perhaps view with most interest the Liberty Horses – most of them of Arab breed – although the Trakehners and the stately Lipizzaners are still in demand, most of those now being used in England are more than three-quarters English thoroughbreds. But the Lipizzaner horses which were seen at Olympia before the Second World War are something more than superb circus performers. This famous breed is of Austrian origin and is so called because of the place, Lipizza, near Trieste, where a stud farm was founded in 1580 by the Archduke Charles, son of the Emperor Ferdinand I. Their actual origins go back to 1564, when the Kladruber (bred on the stud farm of Kladrub in Bohemia), a highly specialised horse – a mixture of Spanish and Neapolitan blood – was introduced into Austria, and crossed with the small horses of Northern Italy. The characteristics of the Lipizzaners are their powerful build but slender legs, small heads, round noses, arched necks and drooping ears. They are rarely over fifteen hands in

124

height and are intelligent and graceful. The beautiful Lipizzaner stallions still draw large crowds of visitors from all over the world to the Spanish Riding School in Vienna, the oldest riding academy in the world.

There used to be magnificent riders among the English tenting shows – the Fossetts, the Paulos, the Bakers and the Yeldings. The Fossetts in particular had a great reputation as riders. The jockey act, which came into existence in early Victorian days, and still holds its own as one of the most spectacular of circus acts, was a family tradition with them. The present Fossett Circus, or, more precisely, one of the three which tented in England and Ireland, still keep Sir Robert Fossett's name. Eighty years ago his father was acknowledged as the champion circus jockey, the winner of countless cups and medals in competitions. Sir Robert had the same reputation which was passed to his son, 'young Robert'. He used to run across the ring with his feet tied in large wicker baskets and with a sack tied over his head, and then jump on a galloping horse.

The horses ridden in the jockey acts are known as 'rosinbacks', derived from the fact that their broad backs are dusted with powdered resin to give the performer foothold. These horses may be of almost any origin and in the old days were often recruited from the shafts of milk vans, butchers' carts and even from the plough.

Two of the most charming acts in the circus ring are 'jumping the balloons and the garters' and the *pas-de-deux*. The balloons are the paper hoops through which the pretty equestrienne jumps and the garters are the coloured streamers on poles which the clowns swing under the horse's feet as the equestrienne makes her jumps. Two performers and two horses take part in the *pas-de-deux*: one performer striding the two cantering animals and swinging his partner into elegant poses.

The Flying Trapeze is more than a century old. It was invented in 1859 by a Frenchman called Léotard. He used two swinging trapezes and two platforms. A graceful and elegant performer, he swung off from one platform while from the other his father sent the second trapeze swinging towards him. At the exact second, Léotard passed from one to the other. He did not use a net, but a long mattress was placed underneath. His début in Paris, at the *Cirque Napoléon*, with this act was such a sensation that he was paid the then fabulous salary of five hundred francs a day.

Léotard was born on 1 August 1838. His father, a gymnastic instructor, kept a school of physical culture at Toulouse; for his son he visualised a respectable career as a lawyer. At the age of eighteen, Léotard, having gained his baccalaureate, gave up the bar for the trapeze. He first appeared in London at the old Alhambra, Leicester Square. Again a tremendous sensation, he received £180 a week to fly through the air over the tables with no net beneath him, and a song was written about him which everyone knows to this day. He returned to Paris and died of smallpox in 1870 soon after having completed the writing of his memoirs. He was only twenty-eight. A number of imitators quickly followed Léotard's appearance at the Alhambra and improved on the apparatus he used. In 1871 the Spanish troupe, the Rizarellis, first used a net; this was at the Holborn Amphitheatre.

But the greatest flying-trapeze artist of all time was Alfredo Codona, the son of a Mexican tenting circus proprietor. He established his act when he was with the Wirth Circus in Australia in 1913, his father then being the catcher. For six seasons Alfredo did a single trapeze act with the Barnum and Bailey show in America, his sister Victoria working on the slack-wire. In 1917 he was performing the flying-trapeze act with his brother Lalo in Havana.

Suddenly he decided that he would achieve what seemed to the whole circus world an impossibility – no less than a triple somersault. Some idea of the foolhardiness of this may be gathered from the fact that at that point in circus history there had been no more than eleven gymnasts who had achieved even the double somersault on the trapeze – nine of them, incidentally, being Frenchmen. The first to accomplish it was Edmond Rainat – who worked until he was eighty – and he was successfully imitated by his brothers Jules and Alexis, by Pierre Bouvier and others.

But the *triple* somersault – no, said Codona's friends, he must forget it. It was suicide. Sometimes a performer did accomplish it, but that was more often than not by accident. This happened to the American clown, Gayton, and he was killed. It happened to Hobbes in London and he was killed. It happened to Dutton, and although he was not killed he was so thankful for his escape that he immediately handed in his notice to the circus management and never went near a circus again.

When Codona resolved to achieve it, Ernie Lane was experimenting with the idea and

Top Con Colleano, 'the Wizard of the Tight Wire', dressed as a matador and performing his Spanish dances in mid-air.

Above Alfredo Codona, one of the greatest trapeze-artists of all time, was famous for the triple somersault which took him three years to perfect.

had come near to success. But at a performance at the Chicago Coliseum, Lane missed his catcher's wrists, fell, hit the edge of the net, and broke his neck. Codona was not to be deterred. At the end of one season he cancelled all his contracts and retired to the Ringling winter quarters to practise and practise. Day after day, week after week, he persisted, sometimes despairing of ever solving the problem of timing which the triple somersault involves. It took him three years to master it and he finally succeeded in putting the fabulous trick into his act at the Chicago Coliseum in 1930. He did not do it every time he tried. His average was nine out of ten, and that still seems to the ordinary trapeze performer a miracle. When Codona did this triple somersault it was estimated that he flew through the air at a speed of sixty miles an hour.

It did not kill Codona but his life was both curious and tragic. He married first Clara Curtin, who worked in the act with him and Lalo. But his second wife was one of the most brilliant circus artists of the time, the great Lillian Leitzel, who was known as the 'Queen of the Circus' and the world's greatest gymnast, the star attraction of the centre ring of Ringling's great American show. An English girl, she had once been one of the Leamy troupe of gymnasts who appeared at the Agricultural Hall, but from America she came to appear at Olympia, no longer a mere member of a troupe but a great star, unsurpassed in her act on the Roman rings.

Her entrance was spectacular. She had dainty feet and exquisitely formed lower limbs and hips which, although they seemed in perfect proportion were really abnormally small for her robustly developed chest and shoulders. But it was a body over which she had an absolute mastery. She entered the ring draped in a white coat, her head crowned with golden hair. Reaching the centre of the ring, she took a toe ballet pose, threw her cloak to the French maid who had followed her and began a slow ascent of the rope, a spotlight picking out her lovely figure as she climbed, the band playing a sentimental slow waltz. Her way of 'rolling' herself up the eighty feet of rope was unique, for she pulled herself up by a series of *planches*. This had only previously been done by male performers and even then it was an exceptional feat of strength, but Lillian Leitzel made it a masterpiece of grace and charm. Her climax was almost incredible, for it consisted in one hundred and fifty giant swings from one arm, an unbelievable test of endurance and strength. Such was the strain of this that on her right wrist was always an open wound. She was told that this wound would eventually result in her death from blood-poisoning, but she merely shrugged her shoulders and went on

Opposite Paulina Schumann of the Schumann Circus on Younouf, a magnificent Arab stallion.

Below Lillian Leitzel, an English trapeze artist of fantastic skill and courage, entertains a street crowd in the 1930s.

with her two daily performances. She must have endured excruciating pain.

Perhaps the best known of modern circus acts has been that of the Wallendas, an act which has since been extensively copied with even more thrills. The Wallendas performed on a high wire stretched one hundred or more feet above the ring; the climax of their act was a miracle of balance, a defiance of danger. The least slip on the part of any one of the four would have brought disaster to all. On a pole stretched from the shoulders of two of the troupe was balanced a chair on which stood a third. On his shoulders stood the top mounter, Helen Wallenda, swaying precariously as the two wire-walkers beneath made their slow and cautious progress along the thin stretch of wire. The limes beat on them, the band played a slow waltz while thousands of eyes watched them. But not of all the audience, for there were always some who could not bear the agony of that slow pushing of the feet along the sagging wire, whose imaginations made them too keenly apprehensive of all that might happen – the sudden slip and the huddle of falling bodies, poles and chair. If the Wallendas had looked down they would have seen far below them midget-like attendants holding a safety net. But that was a sop to the public. The Wallendas had little faith in safety nets. They knew that should the girl fall she would fall outwards, far beyond its reach. And if she fell, the men holding the net would instinctively let go to save themselves from the impact of the twenty-pound balancing poles that would come hurtling down to the ring below.

On one occasion, when they were performing in America, the wire suddenly dipped and sagged as they reached its centre. Carl, in the jerk caused by that unexpected drop, let slip his steel balancing pole. It fell straight for the men holding the net, but they saw it coming and ducked in all directions. At the same time Hermann fell, but clutched the wire with a hand and managed to slip his leg over it. Joseph dropped and hit the rigging wire, he caught desperately at it and got a grip. Carl hurtled downwards from the falling chair; he also contrived to grip the wire. Helen toppled over his shoulder; as she

dropped Carl threw out his legs and, incredible as it may seem, managed to grip her body between his knees. For a few seconds the four hung precariously in mid-air. Then, at a word of command from the ringmaster, the attendants seized the net which they had dropped in their panic and held it tautly in position. One by one the Wallendas dropped to safety. This happened at the afternoon performance. That evening they appeared as if nothing had happened.

The Wallendas were performing in the circus ring when they were children. In their early days they used to do handstands, somersaults, acrobatics and trapeze. But Carl always had a vast ambition to invent a sensational act, something so audacious as to seem impossible. He visualised the wire stretched as high as the circus top would allow. It was an idea originating from the old rope-walkers who would walk a rope stretched from one church steeple to another, but working at this height had not been attempted before in a circus. The act was practised at a height of six feet from the ground. At their second attempt Carl fell on top of Helen, broke his arm and was unable to work for four weeks. He amused himself during this idleness by working out with paper and pencil the details of the act. His arm well, he was eager for practice again. But Helen's nerve had been shaken. 'You're no performer if one fall frightens you,' Carl said contemptuously. Helen was unconvinced. 'Look here,' he added 'do it again and I'll give you a diamond ring!' Helen said she'd try anything for that! And she got the ring. After many months

Above Animal trainer, Egon Widman, of the Mexican Circus, with one of the beautiful and dangerous Bengal tigers.

Opposite This tiger-trainer at Hagenbeck's Circus has perfect command over his charges.

Overleaf A daring young girl on a flying trapeze caught in a spectrum of light.

Following page The Rudolfo Steys performing elaborate set-pieces in mid-air at Billy Smart's Circus.

of incessant practice, Carl considered the act ready. He asked the circus proprietor to let them try it out. The boss would not listen to them. He said he wasn't going to let four young people commit suicide in his circus. Carl wore his patience out and one night the act was given above the ring. It succeeded beyond his greatest expectations and for days letters arrived with offers of contracts.

One night, at a London circus, Helen fainted just as she reached the safety of the platform. It was said that this was a fake, arranged by a press-agent for the sake of publicity. It was not. Some days after Helen remarked: 'Despite what happened, I couldn't give it up. When I'm on the ground again I feel so exhilarated that I don't care. But whenever I see Carl with paper and pencil, then I go cold all over. I'm just scared stiff in case he's thinking out more crazy notions!'

There were two groups of Wallendas, each performing the same act. Willy Wallenda, one of the four of the other act, had two falls; the second resulted in his death. Before this, on the Ringling show, when the troupe were doing their finishing trick, the stakes pulled away from the soft earth and the wire sagged. They did not escape so lightly as the other Wallendas, and it was fortunate that they were not working at their usual

Opposite A spectacular balancing act by trick riders at Billy Smart's Circus.

Above Anxiety is etched on the face of the trainer as he stands surrounded by his beasts.

Right Swiss lion trainer, Catherine Blankart, daughter of a millionaire, drills her troupe of eight lions.

Below Dantes, a lion trainer at the Cirque d'Hiver, puts himself at the mercy of his charges.

height. The result of this mishap was that three of the troupe were in hospital for weeks.

To perform without a safety net has not become a part of many sensational aerial acts. Two acts at Olympia took this risk and both came to grief. Kimri performed on an apparatus shaped like an aeroplane which rotated with increasing speed at a height of one hundred and twenty feet. From an arm of the aeroplane a single trapeze was suspended and on this Kimri performed until one day he fell and was crippled for life. His wife took his place and performed for a considerable time.

An equally dangerous act was Roselle, 'The Man in The Moon', who worked on a silver crescent hung just beneath the top of any circus, no matter what the height. He performed a rotating hand-balance on a curve of the crescent. After appearing at Olympia he went to America and there made one mistake. It was sufficient. Alberty, the German-Swiss, also had a terrifying act, his apparatus being a fifty-foot slender and tapering steel pole with such flexibility that while he climbed it it swayed twenty feet from side to side. On this vibrating pole Alberty performed equilibrist movements, finishing with a handstand. The act may not appear dangerous to an audience but it made circus people shudder.

Perhaps the most astounding of all aerial acts was that of Barbette who entered the ring at Olympia down a flight of stairs, glamorously dressed. After discarding all her clothes except a brassiere and trunks, she proceeded to give a graceful display on the high-wire and then the trapeze. Acknowledging the applause at the climax of her act, she raised her hand to her head and pulled off her blonde wig – to reveal herself as a man. Such was Barbette's success with the act that 'she' went to America for an astronomical salary – only to be killed by overwork.

Most trainers have started by being assistants to others in the same game, so that their nerves are tested from the beginning. Somewhere there must be trainers who have escaped mishap in the circus ring, but if there are any they are few and far between.

Bears are more difficult and dangerous to train than lions and tigers. Here Ursula Boettcher dances with a polar bear at Ringling Brothers, Barnum and Bailey's Circus.

Frank Foster, for many years the ringmaster at some leading circuses, has confessed to knowing of no trainers in his experience who have not suffered some injury at the hands of their charges. So why don't they get out of it, asks Foster, and then goes on to infer that staying in the circus and doing their particular type of job is a drug, and when one is hooked, it's not easy to turn the other way. And in his experience there's not a man-jack amongst trainers who, after some dangerous experience, wishes to place the blame on the animal who has mauled, bitten, nipped, been menacing or run amok.

He tells the story of Priscilla Kayes who was attacked in the cage by Callito, a big male lion a few days after her brother had had an equestrian accident. When her back was turned he jumped from his pedestal, knocked her over, and bit one of her legs. She was on her feet in an instant. The ringmaster shouted and asked if she wanted help. 'I'm all right, Mr Foster,' she said as she was driving the lion back to its pedestal. She then finished the act as if nothing had happened. When she came out of the cage she said to Frank Foster: 'I think you had better look and see if anything is wrong.' The lion's teeth had marked her leg with deep holes, and the doctor who was sent for was astonished at the depth of the wounds he had to plug. An hour later, her leg bandaged, she again went in the cage with her seven lions and performed her act. But the next day she had to give in; stiff and sore and suffering much pain, she had to consult a specialist. It was many weeks before she worked again, but she did so before the end of the season.

Although lions and tigers are often considered the most ferocious of circus animals by

Right High-jumpers from Budapest fly through the air at the Cirque d'Hiver.

Below left Two artists locked together in a spectacular mid-aid somersault.

Below right Trick cyclists at Billy Smart's Circus achieve a miracle of balance and grace.

A human spinning-top at the Moscow State Circus.

the public, circus people know that bears are the most vicious and the most difficult to train, having faulty memories. Luckily they are good travellers and look as if they might be enjoying themselves. Kossmayer was mauled by his polar bear when he was washing it – and the next night the father of the victim was himself in a cage doing his son's act with the same bear, and refusing to have it put down because, as he said, it is never the animal's fault; something happens, an accident; in this case it was – according to Kossmayer Senior – because his son slipped and accidentally knocked the big bear. Then there was Rudolf Matthies, one of the best known trainers of all time, bitten but able to escape the worst of the animal's maulings. He used to show a group of dangerous Bengal tigers, and made the right decision when he married a Hamburg hotel receptionist whilst still middle-aged. With their joint savings he bought land in Germany – and now we suppose they are rearing chickens and pigs. But what of his Bengal tigers? As one modern critic of the circus has said: 'The sawdust and spangles tradition is lovely for human beings who can volunteer for it, but it shouldn't be imposed on animal conscripts.'

Clowns

The word 'clown' seems to derive from the Old Norse *klunni,* meaning loutish. 'The word is cognate with the Danish *kluntet,* clumsy, maladroit, or, in plain Yorkshire dialect, ''proper gormless''', says Eric Partridge in his *Dictionary of Theatrical Terms.*

But there's more to the clown than that, more than a means of filling the gaps in the performances of greater stars. It is true that many clowns are of ephemeral achievement and frequently 'double' in some other act: but the great clown is long remembered and not easily forgotten. *Entrée,* used in the circus sense, is an act of its own which holds the ring for itself. No-one worries about the nationality of this multi-racial figure of fun, as we can see from this account by Thomas Frost of a clown performing in a tent in Turkey in the last century:

> I have said the sight was a curious one, but my surprise was excited beyond bounds when a real clown – a perfect Mr Merriman of the arena – jumped into the ring and cried out, in perfect English: 'Here we are again – all of a lump! How are you?' There was no response to his salutation, for it was evidently incomprehensible; and so it fell flat and the poor clown looked as if he would have given his salary for a boy to have called out 'Hot codlins!' I looked at the bill, and found him described as the 'Grottesco Inglese' Whittayne. I did not recognise the name in connection with the annals of Astley's, but he was a clever fellow, notwithstanding; and, when he addressed the master of the ring, and observed, 'If you please, Mr Guillaume, he says, that you said, that I said, that they said, that nobody had said, nothing to anybody,' it was with a drollery of manner that at last agitated the fezzes, like poppies in the wind, although the meaning of the speech was still like a sealed book.

There are many explanations of laughter. What is it all about? How is it created in the inner-self of the being who creates it in others? People have laughed at the great circus clowns, frequently without knowing why – Popov, Coco, Pimpo, Holloway, Guyon, Auriol, Slater, Oakley, Olschansky, Volkerson, Delprini, Franks, Hogini, Frowde, Keith, Barna, Wallett, Belling, Rice, Toto – whether they appeared alone as a solitary figure, or in troupes – The Fratellinis, The Bronetts, The Rivels, The Price Bros. Once seen, the memory of most of them lingered on.

Who has not watched a knockabout piece of clowning? The throwing of custard pies, the sloshing with buckets of water, often directed by the others at the midget clown, which sometimes nearly drowns the poor fellow, sending him off dripping, spluttering and exhausted. The gallons of water have to be standing by so that there's a non-stop exchange of dough, water and unceasing fun. We're laughing uncontrollably – some of us louder than the kids – reverting to our own childhood.

The trampoline is being tested, the next act is nearly ready, and now all four clowns were thwacking each other, tripping the other up, indulging in bottom-kicking, nose-twisting, soot-spreading on each other's faces. Glue, or is it treacle? Ink, or perhaps blackcurrant jam, white paint that could have been milk, whatever they were doing to each other made the audience laugh at misfortune and thank heaven that the clown in his gooey state was taking the lot. The mirth the clown creates grows in proportion to the humiliation he is forced to endure. More than 'proper gormless' he can be the funniest, as well as the saddest sight any of us have ever seen. Whether it is inherited or acquired, those who are practitioners of the clown's art, like Popov of the Moscow State Circus, have an innate sense of the artistry of the grotesque. Even when the good clown is 'improvising', his teasing, tricking and ad-libbing cannot surprise his fellow clowns. Subconsciously, his studied, rehearsed and concerted act has been 'timed' to the last degree. The surprised reaction of his opposite number is feigned – because they've rehearsed it with him. The audience thinks it's all off-the-cuff, but 'joey' and his fellow clowns, the ringmaster who's seen it all before, as well as the circus proprietor who's booked them in order to see it 'improvised' exactly as before, all know better. To see the great, and not so great, clowns falling upon a certain member of the audience, picking him up, dusting him off with great care and gentleness, taking him back to his seat when the midget clown jumps up again to empty another pail of water down the spectator's shirt, takes the audience in for a moment. Then the victim of this assault runs madly out of the ring and the fact is disclosed that this is the fifth member of the act, rather than a member of an audience, that's now roaring its approval at the indignities inflicted on one of their fellows; albeit a strange, painted, grotesque fellow. And then they look at each other, this remaining quartet of clowns, and as the management now cues them, 'Get off quick – the next's ready – clear!', the figures of fun make a simultaneous grab at the little dwarf. This draws a great unified scream of laughter from the audience as they slap him down, stand him up and slap him down again. They fall, the three of them left in the ring, on their grotesque little partner as he sprawls on his backside. A curious kind of frenzy seizes the trio as they grab their victim, one taking two arms and the others a leg apiece, and as they go off firing loud caps in toy guns and squirting water from pistols, a kind of illogical and vindictive hysteria seizes the laughing audience. The victimised clown is the scapegoat of man; the herdlike fury of the mob can be heaped upon his shoulders and impossible cruelties inflicted upon a deformed victim whose life represents a comic nightmare. Genius and madness, love and hate, tolerance and persecution, beauty and the beast, the clown is man's alter-ego.

Above left and right Musical clowns, Renato, Cluca and Jo-Jo from the German Busch-Roland Circus.

Of course, not all clown acts are funny. So unfunny can they be that Chaplin, who brought clowns into both *Circus* and *Limelight*, made their business sufficiently atrocious by getting all the gags wrong and messing up the routine. Charlie was *the auguste* (which means 'silly fool') to beat all *augustes;* that tramp-like fill-in, who often lends unconscious pathos to a bit when he rushes on between more glamorous acts, unable to get things right or make an impression, falling over ropes, bumping into others, hitching up his baggy trousers, and losing his arm down the lining of his coat.

The real clown – not the *auguste* – normally has his own starred spot today in any circus, and whether he looks like Grock of old or Popov in modern times, he bears more resemblance to the wistful white-faced character in traditional costume, a direct descendant of the Commedia dell'Arte, than he does to the hobo clown who is a knockabout comic.

Despite all the plays, films, novels, anecdotes, 'tall stories', and even song lyrics about the clown with a broken heart – Judy Garland's *Be a Clown,* Gracie Fields' *Laugh, Clown, Laugh,* and *Born to be a Clown, Clown Who Cried, Clown Am I, Death of a Clown, Tears of a Clown, Clown Town, Clown's Painted Smile, Ha, Ha, Said the Clown, Clown in Your Cabaret, Clown Never Cries, Clown and the Bareback Rider, Where are the Clowns?* – there are those versed in circus history who insist that the various deaths, sometimes violent, others in suicide form, of clowns with broken hearts are 'happenings' no more peculiar to the circus than they are to life outside the Big Top:

I wish to emphasise that these accidents, these tragedies, are uncommon; they happen rarely: they are not, and never will be, a commonplace of the circus. And although I have once seen an acrobat fall, I have *never* – and I know many artists – encountered that intolerable bore, The Clown With a Broken Heart.

Admittedly that was written some years ago and many 'On With the Motley' tragedies have to our certain knowledge been enacted in the meantime. But was Frank Foster – a famous ringmaster in his day – correct in writing as he did even then? The star turn of any circus, the First Clown, has always taken precedence over the aerialist, the lion-

Above The most famous clown act in Europe for a long time was that of Paul, Francois and Albert Fraţellini, who were the great attraction at the Cirque Medrano in Paris. Sadly, their only visit to London was a flop.

Opposite above Galettis the Swiss clown, wearing the absurd baggy trousers of the traditional auguste, performs in Denmark.

Opposite below Two clowns struggle to pull a cracker with an impassive poodle.

144

tamer, the herds of elephants, even the beautiful showgirls of the modern American circus. It is the clown who can make or break a circus by the tricks he does, his presence, personality, his gaiety in the ring and the mystique of his sadness out of it. Almost impossible to analyse such clownery – its likeness to a combination of tears and laughter, the latter inside the enclosed world of the circus, the former in the tragic theme that has haunted so many clowns, *augustes* and joeys in their private lives. Mr Foster was not completely unaware of this fact when he wrote in the same book, *Clowning Through,* of the comic Sam Pugh:

> All his accomplishments, together with his knowledge of music, allied to an histrionic talent which never failed him, should have made him one of the most prominent figures of his time. Here was a clown, admired by his fellow performers, every difficult aim in the circus achieved, who never gained the popularity he deserved, and who died in a workhouse . . .

There is a sharp distinction between the laughter directed *at* animals performing human tricks and the laughter *with* clowns who are simply being human – those figures of fun who have schizophrenic personalities and lead dual lives that down the years have made the description 'Broken-Hearted Clown' more fact than fantasy. Take 'Little Walter', a famous Belgian clown (Walter Ulrich Alaxandre) who died at Castelo Branco in circumstances of great poverty. He had gone to Lisbon at the turn of the century, and year after year, until the First World War, he was the King of Clowns, the embodiment of clownery. His voluminous check suit, the lank red hair and bulbous nose, his antics and patter (in broken Portuguese) were the joy of a whole generation, young and old. Afterwards, at the war's end, there was a decline in circus popularity and the 1920s saw the rising star of another sort of clown – the screen clowning of Chaplin. Little Walter seemed to fade away. Broken in health and fortune, he tried to pick up his former position, but the 1930s found him in Portugal where he had been touring for the last few years, sinking ever lower in the hierarchy of clowns. By 1937 he was dead: working in a fitup show in the provinces. They said of Little Walter that he died surrounded by his wife and children, who were all in the circus with him. If this is true, then a larger than (even circus) life portrait can be painted – one that depicts tiny

Four clowns have difficulty in putting out a fire which has started in the hat of an oblivious fifth.

acrobats, circus riders, lion-tamers, performing bears, ringmaster, daring trapeze artists and jugglers, joining the penniless clown's widow to attend the last moments of one they called 'Little Walter' who had been Great.

Marceline, another clown of international renown, was found dead in New York nearly fifty years ago, with a bullet in his brain. His real name was Isadore Orbes, and he was a Spaniard who had made the USA his home after successful appearances at the London Hippodrome; but in the 1920s he found his clowning out of date, opted out of the circus with his earnings of thirty years, and managed to lose everything he had ever earned in setting himself up as an impresario, a producer of night club shows in Greenwich Village, N.Y. When they found the old clown's body – for he was never a born entrepreneur, and a circus feeling clung to him to the end – they saw beside him a pawnticket for a diamond ring. His last possession was six dollars in cash.

It was in Paris that 'Pappy' the dwarf clown from Hungary paid his hotel bill before going to his bedroom. There he rang the bell for room service, ordered a tankard of beer, and told the chambermaid who brought it to keep the change from the note he tossed to her. When the door had closed he drank his beer – and hanged himself. Pappy was fifty-three. Not old for a clown by circus standards in those days certainly, but his partner a score of years older, Gogo, had recently been forced to retire. Their bill-matter had been 'Gogo and Pappy'; now it was just 'Pappy-the Clown' on his own. Without his more energetic partner in clownery he could not find a job for himself and the prospects looked too black to go on. They buried him in a tiny coffin, just big enough to hold his 3ft 7in body. The half-a-dozen clowns from a nearby circus took their little pal's remains to a cemetery just outside Paris, but this was out of respect for the past; in the present the strength of only one of their number was sufficient to carry the coffin to its last resting place.

They came from everywhere and settled anywhere, these clowns: Gabriel, although Russian-born was British-naturalised, and one day he had left his mean suburban lodging outside Paris to search for work as a film extra in the studios where, ironically, they were making a film about the circus. No real circuses were scheduled until early spring; now it was November and a long winter lay ahead for the workless and hungry clown. The number of 'extras' required had been taken on for the day's shooting and

Below left and right Famous American clown, Lou Jacobs, struggles out of his miniature car, a favourite clown gag.

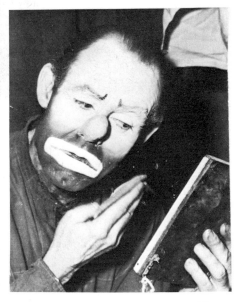

had there been a fire to go back to in his little carpetless room Gabriel would have walked the five miles 'home' and with no food in his belly would have crept between the covers that passed for bedclothes. Only the underground railway was warm and on this autumn day the fifty-two-year-old clown, without a living soul in the world to care whether he lived or died, walked into the station entrance, down the stairs to the platform – and waited. When Gabriel leapt to his death as the train lurched round the bend before stopping at the platform it was as spectacular an act – this last performance of the unwanted clown – as anything he'd done under the Big Top when he had joined as deputy Les Fratellinis, when one of their number had died. He was good, too, was Gabriel, and he stayed on with the remaining members until they retired and he was left to plod on alone. A score of years younger than the others, he had only memories instead of either retirement or work. Life had once been good . . .

They used to call Sabatini 'The Great Sabatini'. But that was when he earned over £100 per week (a star's salary in the 1920s) and his name flared from circus posters in London, Paris and New York. Sabatini the Clown! The Great Sabatini! Audiences throughout the world paid to see him in their thousands, for his ability to raise their laughter turned his talent into gold. But like other stars before (and after) him The Great Sabatini was forgotten long before he died. To London's theatre and film queues waiting to see other stars of stage and screen came the elderly clown, the circus 'back number' turned street busker, and performed in a hard road rather than a circus ring, to a long line of only half-interested audiences instead of those keenly attentive ones who had applauded the art of the circus clown when they surrounded him in a magic circle. Now, trying to amuse the potential customers with a hat on the pavement at his feet to receive their tributes for his efforts in the form of pennies and halfpennies, he had adopted another name for his present inferior act. He had re-christened himself 'Pop Gintano' – and it was as Pop Gintano that the Great Sabatini was in due course removed from his bare little Soho garret to the nearby Charing Cross Hospital. Ill-luck, lack of food, a poor response to his 'act' from a new-style audience to whom Sabatini was unknown, an inability to pay his latest rent demand had caused a collapse when he returned after midnight and, along with the tablets from a small bottle that had overturned on a chair next to his camp bed, was the tiny pile of money he'd collected that night – four shillings, in that era's currency, in all. It was said later that the insignificant busker 'Pop' would sometimes go out to collect pieces of stick from the gutter to build a fire for himself on the hearth in his room. Cracks in the wall were stuffed up with old papers to keep out the draughts, and upon many occasions 'Pop' had been forced to buy a handful of tapioca to feed himself for the day. The old chap was still unconscious when they locked the door on a room to which he would never return. No photos or playbills that served to remind him of his former glory ever decorated the bare walls of that new world of anonymity. They took him now to an even newer world; of hospitals; an adjunct to that other 'existence' The Great Sabatini had endured since leaving the circus. He long ago forgot a world that had forgotten him.

And so they continue, these stories of famous and unknown clowns, lucky and unlucky clowns, funny and unfunny clowns, unhappy but very rarely happy clowns. They are peculiar folk and their courage is monumental. Circus folk often start clowning when over sixty; then with more specialised careers in the ring not open to them because of age and the greater agility that's needed to be trainer, aerialist, juggler or bareback rider, they become quite often 'carpet' clowns and some of them live to a great age. Cavilla, the clown, was entertaining the kids in a circus in a park in Albany, New York, and was back-somersaulting at the age of a hundred. He lived to be over 105. Poodles, the Yorkshire horseback clown, was another who was still known as 'The Riding Fool' – walking off the back of a horse, racing round the ring at high speed – in his seventy-fifth year and who kept on the job of being a clown to the last. Coco, a brilliant clown in his day, was fifty-eight years old – a Latvian turned Briton, and fighter (as well as clown) during the last war – when for a few hundred odd pounds the Inland Revenue made him bankrupt. Living in a caravan, abstemious, his only luxury a television set, this veteran clown who brought happiness to millions in his day was crippled at the end in a road accident. Courageous to the last he founded a road-safety scheme for the benefit of his beloved young audience of the past, to ensure that they would be protected from the bad drivers on the highways. For his zeal and social sense Coco is specially remembered. He was a mere stripling (for a clown) of seventy-three when he died during a successful comeback, honoured – who better – before he died in

Opposite Emmett Kelly transforms his face for the 'Weary Willie' tramp clown figure who delighted audiences at Ringling Brothers, Barnum and Bailey's Circus.

Above Four members of Clown Cavalcade, a school for professional clowns, experiment with different types of clown make-up. A code of the circus forbids copying of make-up so that each clown's face is unique.

Left Coco, a Latvian whose real name was Nicolai Poliakoff, was for many years a favourite figure at Bertram Mills Circus. Here his real face contrasts his made-up face, showing how he built up his false nose.

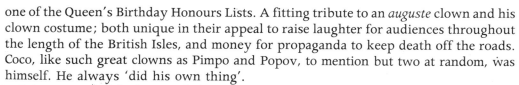

Opposite A sad face behind the clown's smiling make-up.

Overleaf bottom A group of clowns in their dressing room.

Overleaf top left A colourful clown from a German circus.

Overleaf top right Coco the clown gets ready to step out in his famous big shoes.

Below Coco the clown was honoured in the Queen's Birthday Honours List, but ended his days in relative poverty.

Right Ron and Sandy Severini, a husband-and-wife clown team who delight American audiences.

one of the Queen's Birthday Honours Lists. A fitting tribute to an *auguste* clown and his clown costume; both unique in their appeal to raise laughter for audiences throughout the length of the British Isles, and money for propaganda to keep death off the roads. Coco, like such great clowns as Pimpo and Popov, to mention but two at random, was himself. He always 'did his own thing'.

It is inconceivable that we shall ever see two clowns' faces made up in precisely the same way. Every clown invents his own face, and however much it may appear similar to others, it is never identical; for there is a code of the circus that permits no copying of makeup. There are the classical formulas naturally, but apart from the *entrée* of clowns, the carpet clowns, the circus clowns, the *augustes* and the joeys, who are instantly recognisable to those familiar with stock characters in the circus, the makeups – and frequently the costumes – are like finger prints in their dissimilarity; sometimes evident and quite obvious, at other times only subtly contrasted and hardly noticeable until one puts the two *augustes* or joeys together, side by side; then, like the alleged 'identical' twins, one can detect the difference, however minute it may be.

The funny man has always swamped his foremost rivals because he moves laughter from the heart. For example Popov, of the Moscow State Circus, has concentrated upon conveying a human and realistic performance in every clown he plays. For he avers that modern audiences demand to see *natural* men who are funny, rather than degenerates, paralytics, idiots and stock depictions of caricatures, even allowing for the parody of the circus we've been led to expect. Popov quotes L. Tanti's book, *The Soviet Circus*, written in 1933 – when Popov was a little boy – to support

his plea for all red-haired clowns to be men; even when they are gay dogs, nitwits, gasbags, muddlers and thieves. One can only respect the feelings of Popov for his fellow men when he demands that 'the chief thing for every circus artist, in whatever kind of act, is the high dignity of man which must be shown in the ring of any modern circus'. A laudable sentiment and in keeping with the great artists, but such a humourless approach to humour is sometimes inclined to foul up the works when the depicter is an artist of minimal talent. Humour is not always open to analysis – ask the great Chaplin, Leno's and Robey's ghosts (if our reader is a spiritualist); ask some of the great instinctive actors and actresses, who are natural comedians, whether one can ever have schools for comedy. 'Timing' is subconscious knowledge but dependent upon both intuition and instinct, allied to experience. Working hard to be perfect is often necessary, perhaps invariably necessary, but all the work in the world cannot make an unfunny man (or woman) funny unless they have a funny bone, an ability to 'time' and, even when humourless offstage or away from the arena, a feeling for the humour of the situation or the characterisation in performance itself. Clown Schools are fine for the Popovs of this world – like the drama schools of the theatre – but neither can help the student to achieve ultimate success unless there is the latent talent to create and foster and 'play-in' and polish. And it must be remembered by the Great Popov, as it was remembered by the Great Grock, that rigid rules about what is funny and what is good for audiences are, and in our view must remain, matters of opinion. The great comics are felt to be funny anywhere – with or without training schools.

The technically brilliant and keenly intelligent Popov, arguably – with Grock – the finest clown of the lot – certainly in modern times, for we never saw Rice, Burt, Grimaldi, is still comparatively young. He is the other side of the coin to the broken-hearted clowns we've written about already. He's worked it out and brought a rare perfection to his art of circus clowning in a great modern circus. He is the first *modern* clown of the circus and as such commands our warmth and respect. He is forever on the change, on the run to experiment, ever different, splendidly versatile, hugely disciplined (as one would expect of a Moscow State Circus principal clown) and refreshingly humble about his craft and admiring of others. His hero-worship of Chaplin, for instance, shows a true humility that can only be extended by one great

Top right and left Grock, one of the most gifted and best-known clowns in the history of the circus. The son of a poor inn-keeper, he was a shrewd businessman and at the end of his life owned a luxurious, lake-side mansion in Switzerland. One of his most popular acts was to produce a tiny violin from an enormous case.

Above Oleg Popov, the star attraction of the Moscow State Circus.

artist towards another and denotes true self-awareness. This, clearly, is what Popov possesses – and unless he is demoted, leaves the State Circus, or has a radical change of character, he will continue to salute greatness in others. While he's being subsidised, he'll not concern himself too deeply with the mad scramble for success, the rivalry that makes all overcrowded professions such a rat race. We've never met Popov, nor for that matter is there much need to. It's the artist underneath the mask that counts in our reckoning. But from the way he writes, the manner in which he applies himself to his job, the talent we saw upon more than one occasion when he honoured England with his brilliant presence, he is doubtless a splendid fellow: a clown hardly likely to die of a broken heart. He is 'secure' now, still not old, recognised, blessed with a true philosophy, an artist of great finesse. He graces the circus, and audiences – wherever he plays – are the better for having seen his modernity.

Grock, who one of the present writers first saw at the Brighton Hippodrome in the 1920s, was the *circus* clown supreme. He started in the sawdust ring and his last appearance – five years before he died, at the age of seventy-nine – was in the Hamburg Circus, on 31 October 1954. Grock was no conscious philosopher, offstage or out of the ring, his whole life was spent in being the greatest clown of the lot and giving the same performance – ever fresh, ever novel, seemingly improvised (which it wasn't), a truly original work of art – because his worldwide public insisted upon his act staying precisely as it was. But although his was 'the art that concealed art' and gave every circus-artist-called-clown who has ever lived since, including Popov, an object lesson in how to do it without self analysis in print or lecture, it is certain that Grock himself gave more credit to his flair for 'self advertisement and publicity' than he ever did to his remarkable talent. He was a great 'public relations man' was Grock; long before they had *that* kind of PR, (outside Barnum of course, who beat the drum for others he presented as well as himself). Individuality was of course his particular metier. Hard

Left and right and opposite left Oleg Popov performing his slack-wire routine at the Moscow State Circus. Probably the greatest and most individual clown of modern times, he has rejected the traditional clowning style in favour of a more subtle and naturalistic approach.

work? His own secret. He was of the opinion that there was something more to it when he pronounced in an interview in 1930:

> As I have said elsewhere, I have known clowns who are as good as I am, if not better, but I have never known any who knew how to get on as well as I did. Talent and efficiency go without saying, but that is not enough. The world has to be told by a process of suggestion that this especial piece of work deserves its attention, but never show the world that one needs it. Be as modest as possible in one's own requirements, but never appear to be modest, and especially never display poverty. People dislike those who appear poor, because it makes them feel uneasy. However hungry I was, I always acted as though I did not need anybody's help. I know what it is not to have money, and what it means to keep money when you have it . . .

Yet for all this slightly chilling candour, 'The emperor of all clowns' – as Priestley called him – could be depressed. He was sitting one day in a beer garden looking so sad and isolated from the crowd around him that the waitress, about to serve her forlorn customer asked whether there was anything the matter to make him look so sad. The clown's face off-duty looked more tragic than ever and the wave of melancholia overwhelmed the kindly waitress as a wintry crease appeared, so austere it could never have passed for a smile, and the dejected mouth opened and shut to murmur 'I'm *very* depressed'. An understatement thought the waitress as she went on her way. Minutes later bringing back the meal for her customer, the world's greatest clown, whom she failed to recognise without his make-up, she said with a forced cheerfulness, as though to cheer up this poor, sad, neglected and depressed figure, 'Grock's playing in the circus here tonight. Why don't you go to see him? He'll cheer you up, if nobody else will'. And Grock buried his head in his beer mug and grew smaller and more deflated than ever . . .

It was Grock's special genius that there was no other clown like him. He could not be

Akram Yusupov in the ring of the Tashkent State Circus.

reproduced exactly, unless to give a physical impersonation is to be taken to be precisly like one's subject. We might laugh at the mimic, and if he has something behind the gift of impersonation as an addition to reinforce his talent in behaving like somebody else we might laugh a lot, but creating laughter and tears in abundance – and Grock did both – has more to it than merely going through the motions and following somebody else's creativity. He was a great original, was Grock, who started in the circus and finished in the circus – in between he played the halls, the cabarets, the concerts maybe, and was headlined wherever he went, playing in palaces to the crowned heads of Europe and the masses whose God he was – for basically he was a circus clown. We were his helpless slaves in laughter and his greatness was magnified by our being made to feel that we were laughing at a mime who did it all in error, for he was never trying – so we fondly thought – to make us laugh.

And Grock's tale, from rags to riches, faded in conventional happiness; although it is doubtful whether the circus clown who ended as he started – in the circus ring – ever thought of it like that. He was praised for the wrong things he thought; in his own opinion he was more 'a brilliant man of business – the loyal taxpayer' than he was the great clown. That's what he wanted to hear. And when they took him from his great Swiss mansion, more like a giant museum on a lake with its forty-odd bedrooms and dignified splendour, his farewell to life was vastly different from that of so many other joeys. Flags flew at halfmast, leader columns in the world press paid homage, and his refusal to explain his mastery of clownery was remembered. 'My tricks', he once said 'arrive to me by what the gamesters call luck and the poets inspiration'. What we have – those of us who ever had the chance of seeing Grock – is the legacy he left to us of being able to lord our superiority tantalisingly over the youth of today when we murmur: 'Ah, but *you* never saw Grock.'

There have been clowns since man first recognised in himself and his neighbour the

Below The legendary figure of the sad clown. Chabri, the French clown, in pierrot's costume, sits alone at the end of the show.

Opposite Crippled in a road accident, Coco launched a road safety campaign for the benefit of his young audiences. Here he talks to a little girl who is holding his Belisha beacon walking-stick.

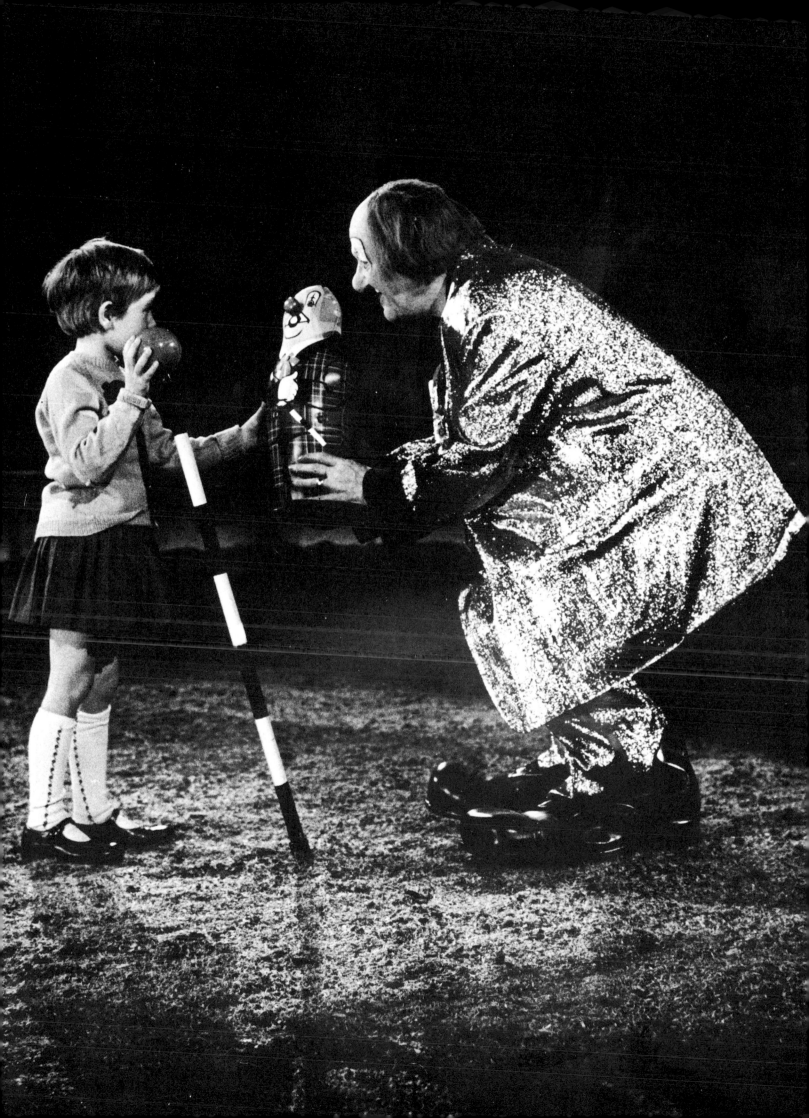

impulse to laugh cruelly at ill-luck. The savagery of the laughter it first aroused gave place to affection; what had originally been natural ill-luck became assumed grotesqueness until, with the development of the modern circus, came its own family of clowns of the highest pedigree if not of unbroken line: the *entrée* clown, then the *auguste* – and finally, up until our own time, the joey. Now *in* our own time comes the Charlie. 'He's a proper Charlie' has become common usage; slang, if you like, but as apt and expressive of the dilapidated but benevolent ape as Grock's clown used to be – or Chaplin's clown, that other 'Charlie', with a protective regard for his own dignity that warmed our hearts in the midst of his tribulation and caused laughter to mix with sympathy. And others too numerous to mention, old and young clowns, few of them rich clowns, all of them clowns who've brought some (many of them, much) gaiety to their fellows, some of them clowns with broken hearts at the end of hard and self-sacrificing lives. The tragic lost-love stories, the financial embarrassments, the oblivion for some and penury for others; many endings bear a striking similarity to what we are so often told are 'old wives' tales'. They are certainly not for the young although the laughter of children once made merry the burial of Kenedi, a sixty-two year old Hungarian clown, who died suddenly in a railway carriage. In accordance with the terms of his will, sorrow was banished from Kenedi's funeral. And to the accompaniment of cheering children the clown's fellow-artists gave a performance by the open grave. They turned somersaults, juggled with plates and balls, swallowed swords, played the banjo. His best friends wore clown costumes – with their faces painted white and daubed with spots of colour. They wore peaked caps with bells that rang as they shook their heads to hide their tears.

Opposite A clown at the Cirque Medrano, Paris, prepares for his act.

Above Three different types of clown in Fellini's film *Clowns*, all sad, contrast with the archetypal children's friend, exemplified here by Otto Griebling of Cole Brothers Circus (1935).

The Cult of the Circus

Above Two Little Circus Girls, painted in 1879 by Jean Renoir.

Opposite bottom left L'Arlequin Rose by C. Lagar, 1925. Petit Palais, Geneva.

Opposite bottom right The Clown by Bernard Buffet, 1955. Petit Palais, Geneva.

Opposite top Two studies of clowns by Mervyn Peake.

Overleaf Performing dogs in a German circus.

At one time it was the 'spectacular' aspect of circuses that appealed to people. The '*Great* Parade of Elephants', '*Scores* of Liberty Horses', '*Varied and Many* Troupes of Circus Clowns', '*Grand* Wild West Show' scenes, inserted as special extras into the general performance, helped to draw the crowds. Today, although tradition dies hard, the circus is more sophisticated on the surface – and if it's not the identical same as in the past, there is no reason why it should be. Different times create different demands and changed tastes. But all audiences from the mobs and courts of Ancient Rome down to the followers of Astley (Barnum, Hagenbeck, Wirth, Chipperfield, Boswell-Wilkie, Krone and Knie), and right on to the present, are fascinated by the achievements of those who do wondrous acts of daring; are smitten with uncontrollable mirth by those who use elaborate contraptions and gags; and experience mass psychological reaction to the roll of drums, the hooves of galloping horses, the whip's crack and the shrill blast of an equestrian's whistle. This is *special* magic; not theatrical magic (of which in these days there is all too little to satisfy the public's craving for escape into another world of warmth, colour, skill and fun), nor film, balletic, operatic and musical magic, but *circus* magic: entering our bloodstream it races our hearts as the general lights dim, the spots flash on, the parade starts to the accompaniment of the rousing march; and as the show gets into its stride all the outer world of reality fades from the mind of the circus audience: that collective thing that is like no other audience in the world. The circus is potentially teeming with life even today. Let there be no dispute about that, though there are those eager to say that it is dying. It has certainly had to face the onslaught of many rivals, but as the novelty wears off its competitors the dance and Bingo halls and skeeball alleys, and the 'nine-days'-wonder' becomes as much a commonplace as the telly in the corner, the dishwasher and the washing machine, the circus that has foundered regains its status and attracts by its magnetism those for whom a 'trip' means something other than being a drug addict. Neither a television-minded press, nor devastating wars abroad, nor cutbacks, recessions and almost weekly economic disasters that affect the whole entertainment industry can kill Circus.

The average child's fascination for the circus is marvellous to behold. On long and generous programmes it is possible to watch the children who squat on narrow forms near the ring fence. One we saw was not more than four years old, and there were no parents visibly with him, only a cluster of slightly older brothers and sisters. He was watching the ring, his small face flushed with rapture, fixed in an expression of such happiness that the smile seemed a part of him. His hands were clapping, slowly and gently, moving apart and together in a rhythm out of his own consciousness. He had

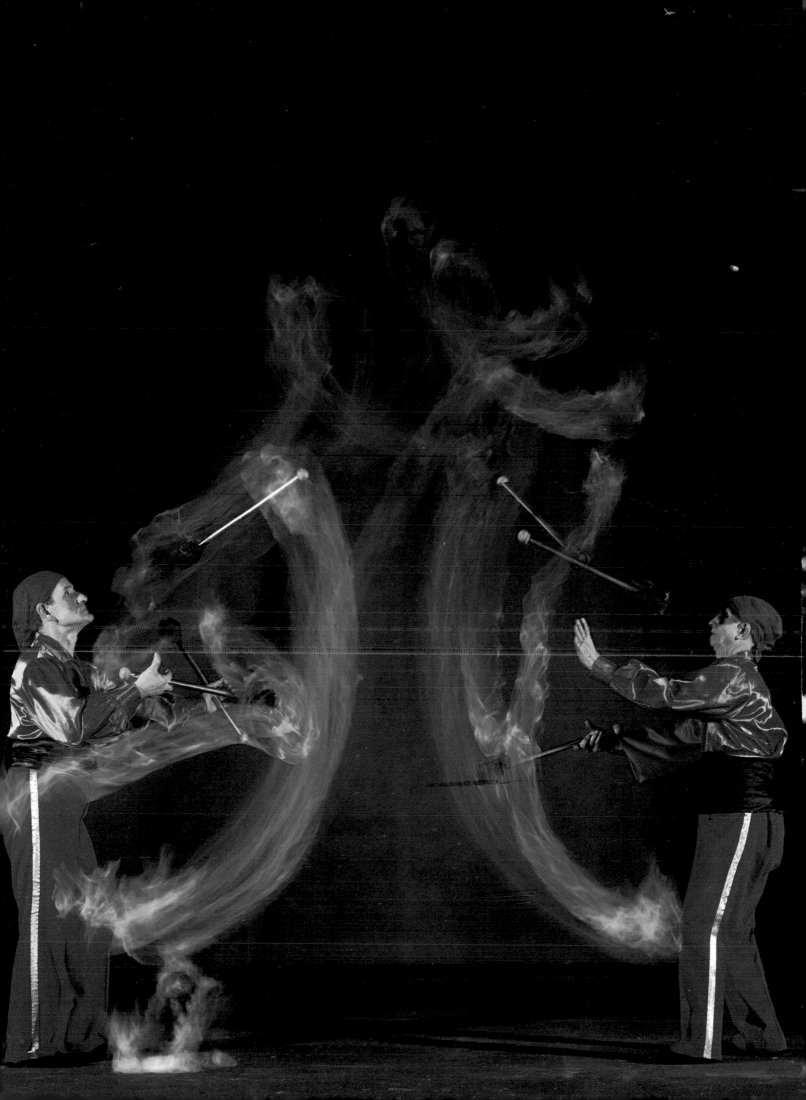

Previous colour pages A family of acrobats form a human pyramid and jugglers make firey patterns in the air.

Previous page Amateur Circus by James Tissot (1836-1902).

Above Bareback Riders, painted in 1886 by W. H. Brown.

forgotten he was clapping, forgotten his brothers and sisters and the other children, forgotten his existence. Only his eyes went greedily in pursuit of more colour, more movement, more comedy. We shall think of him whenever we hear the appeal of the circus questioned, whenever its tradition is called into doubt. If he had sat alone on the benches, instead of being one of several hundred deliriously happy children, the effort of the performance would have been justified.

Indeed, what a galaxy of talent and distinction, artistic and regal, this art for the masses has attracted; as well as that small boy at the circus and the hundreds of thousands of children who rock with laughter and get transported to another world just as he did, it is interesting to remember that Queen Victoria and Dickens were inveterate lovers of the circus, as were painters like Toulouse-Lautrec, Renoir, Seurat, and Picasso, musicians like Mark Hambourg and Joseph Szigeti, and many, many writers.

Why do we, the adults, love the circus? Can it be that sense of danger – for others? A feeling not only for the galloping horses, the smell of countless animals, the brass bands that play the waltzes by Baynes and the marches by Souza, the fun of the clowns and the skill and daring of the performers? From Moscow, Berlin, Amsterdam, Hamburg, Stockholm and Paris come the headline acts that make danger a feature and have the crowds yelling one moment and hardly daring to breathe the next, like the primitive spectacles, still seen today in the bull-rings of Spain, and at certain 'privileged' centres all over the world, where the obscene 'entertainment' of cock-fighting takes place: the ritual blood-letting, the sadistic feeling latent in so many that has to be catered for in so many different ways. Naturally, no circus proprietor or producer wants to see any casualties at the circus; but a latent desire in others for blood letting or at least an 'experience' as in ancient times, might well live on. Is one's excitement whetted by the knowledge that there is no net to catch the victim of a slip if a strand breaks or a step is missed? Nets are not used all the time in certain circuses and, if the authorities decide that the time may come when to use a net is compulsory for all circuses, would the thrill have died and the 'draw' of the circus gradually evaporate at the box office?

Yet surely some of the fascination the circus holds for many is its never-changing nature, its refusal to become truly modern and progressive? It might be nonsense to suppose that of those drawn to the circus, the majority have been motivated by a desire to see cruelty inflicted on others. It is less open to doubt that, with the possible exception of Artaud's Theatre of Cruelty, any other entertainment has remained so static down the years. And the overpraised Artaud is no innovator of styles, much of the Elizabethan stage being a cesspit shambles. Neighbour to Shakespeare's Globe theatre was the highly commercial Bear Garden, with its torture; drama's 'props' were severed heads with mutilations and slaughter abounding. Perhaps the modern circus proprietor in order to keep up with the headlines in the papers, the 'blackest' comedy in the cinema and theatre in which *all* is allowed, merely needs to prove that he is a traditionalist in his tastes and practices? Blood and guts were after all the attraction in the ancient circus.

Yet, beyond this sense of daring and chance, the skill exhibited by the performers on view and the general appeal of the ring and the lights, the music and the decor, the smell of the animals and the general sensation felt by the followers of a fascinating and sometimes disturbing spectacle, could surely have to do with the constant loyalty this cult finds in many followers. Nearly every country has a circus fans' association to propagate the virtues of the life that's led by the folk who still go in for tenting, and few of those who have followed circuses – a common practice in many countries of the 'tent followers' as they've been dubbed – are able to keep away from the Big Top. Even when the latter is only a small Big Top affair. Intoxicating all who enter are the odour of the dens, straw, sawdust, sweating horses, tan and canvas, together with the noises of the whispered encouragement to the animals and the typical circus music playing during performances, the silence of tense audiences when exceptional daring is being executed up high and the roar of approval and sometimes thunderous applause when a trick's been completed and relief is felt at the safe return to the ring from the highest wire. The glare and glitter of lamps and flares and boom spots and thousands of little electric light bulbs, of greasepaint, sequins, clown's garbs, spangles, fleshlings is forever up your nose and in your hair as well as in your eyes: that intangible *something* that gets into your bloodstream for ever and exercises an authority upon its victim that you are unwilling to part with. The senses are affected, your judgment is affronted – and altogether participation in circus life makes for willing slavery.

Unlike Barrie's Peter Pan, the Circus has never asked its public to 'believe in fairies'.

Above In the Wings, pastel drawing by Toulouse-Lautrec.

Left Charlie Chaplin in a scene from his film *The Circus*.

167

Its history has been written with sweating charioteers, trapeze artists, lions and tigers, troupes of elephants and the invariable clowns, rather than with lost boys and pirates. It has asked you to hold your breath rather than clap your hands; knowing full well that the excited cheers, as in Ancient Rome, will come in due course without any entreaty upon any performer's part other than a small gesture of acknowledgement at the end of a trick or the completion of an act.

'First impressions,' said Barrie – again in *Peter Pan* – 'are very important'. Perhaps this is why the nostalgia we all have for entertainment in the past makes us receptive to entertainment in the present. For if children look back upon their brief lives, in much the same way that their elders do upon their long lives, they are surely capable of remembering how it felt to want the noise and splendour to go on and on. Nor is it unlikely that those still youthful ones, who recall the splendour of the Olympia and Harringay circuses when they were *very* young, and their elders were not *so* old, suffer also from nostalgia? In the provincial centres of the U.S. especially, the parade advertising its arrival was always a matter of joyful anticipation for the inhabitants of any city into which the circus marched: with a 'Hold your horses, the Circus is here!' as a grand introductory slogan, declaiming the obvious fact that the clowns on stilts were there, as were the elephants in full force, the wild beasts in cages on top of carts and the brass band playing Souza's 'Anchors Aweigh' or 'The Stars And Stripes'; keeping time to which all the circus folk (tent-fitters, stake hitters, ringmaster, acts and menagerie attendants) would march in procession. Not only the youngsters but their elders and the old folk would raise a cheer and feel exhilarated by the arrival of the show and the knowledge that they would see shortly yet another grand display; brought to town, this time, by one of the country's many travelling circuses. Nowadays it happens more rarely and since the Ringling Brothers, Barnum and Bailey circus decided in the mid 1950s to become an arena-style show and not under the Big Top, the circus enthusiasts

A galaxy of talent in Cecil B. de Mille's film *The Greatest Show on Earth*, 1952.

out of the cities have felt deprived of what was once considered to be typical *American* entertainment. It wasn't, of course; Astley's came before the American Circus (and then several centuries after the Romans) – but that didn't matter; it was essentially 'grassroots' stuff for many and the native patriotism of the small, as well as large, towner, was chronicled by writers like Mark Twain, with affection and perception as well as with that endearing and gentle wit that went to make him unique. Today in the 'sticks' there are over thirty circus families still travelling around a vast continent in truck caravans and using tents. Whilst such activity continues, and there are expeditions to all parts of the States and Canada by various companies showing under the Big Top, few Americans can honestly feel that circus, albeit in a different form, has entirely disappeared.

Edmund Kean, later a great actor, was a youthful strolling player of fifteen when he joined Saunders' circus, where in the performance of an equestrian feat he fell and broke his leg. He left St Bartholomew Fair, where the circus was showing, never to return. Had this accident not occurred perhaps Master Kean, 'bareback rider', or even a clown, would have ended his days in a circus and been one of a long line of 'joeys' now forgotten. Instead he was to become the country's leading tragedian, although the circus must have rubbed off on him, for he was later described by Coleridge: 'Seeing him act was like reading Shakespeare by flashes of lightning' and by Talma: 'a magnificent uncut gem; polish and round him off and he will be a perfect tragedian'. For both references could provide an insight into the former life of the dissolute genius who was upon occasion to ride his horse (bought from a circus and christened Shylock) throughout the night. He was 'presented' with a tame lion with which he might be found playing in his drawing-room. The prizefighter Mendoza, as well as many circus folk, were his constant companions for much of his life.

The magnet has been for others, besides writers, painters and social workers . . .

Below left Students at Florida State University perform an aerial act.

Below right Students at Sylvia de Montfort's school for circus and mime in Paris, set up in emulation of schools in Eastern Europe, and held in an old music-hall.

In fact, circus life has always attracted potential entertainers, and many stars of stage and screen have started their careers as entertainers under the Big Top. Wallace Beery remained two years as an arena assistant. Burt Lancaster, who achieved one of his biggest successes as a trapeze artist in the film *Trapeze,* had, like Beery, worked behind the scenes of a show. Ken Maynard was first attracted by the active adventurous life of circus folk and at the age of fourteen ran away from home to join a touring wagon company. In 1923 he rode for Ringling Brothers Circus and his sensational act with this company ultimately led to a big screen career. Tom Mix, the most famous film cowboy of the lot, didn't stay long in a circus but got his early training in one, and in passing through married – for the fifth time – Mabel Hubball, well-known trapeze artist, known as 'Mabel Ward'. Later, Mix bought a circus and so died in harness. Lydia Roberti was the daughter of a famous circus clown, with whom she travelled for most of her childhood. Hal Skelly, a one-time Broadway star actor, had joined a circus before leaving school; running away one day he joined a travelling troupe; years before he ever saw the playhouse his platform was the sawdust ring. Ford Sterling was one of 'the Flying Leos' a little known act in tenting shows all over America, and after five years of this stint he went into the Keystone Cops, the Mack Sennett comedies. Another circus tourist was Richard Talmadge, the serial stunt star, who toured with his showman father in a circus act known as 'The Metzetti Brothers'. Robert Williams was another kid who played truant from school and joined a circus at the age of ten. Richard Hearne's father was an acrobat and for two years – between 1918 and 1920 – the comedian who was to become known as the acrobatic star of the English musical stage, 'Mister Pastry', toured in the circus with him. Bonar Colleano jnr. made his first appearance as an infant with Ringling Brothers Circus, San Francisco. Comic stars of stage and film, Billy Merson and Bud Costello, were among many other graduates from tent shows. For these performers perhaps the life-under-canvas answered dreams, as well as ambitions, that were only finally realised when they left the sawdust ring for greater fame.

For most folk, throughout the world, the circus conjures up an adventurous world beyond the ken of ordinary lives and when the circus is on show, whether in the big cities and capitals of the world or in the hick dates way out West, in the Montmartre of Paris, or Hamburg, the German 'home' of the Circus, audiences everywhere are prepared to suspend disbelief, to indulge in their love of fantasy. Over it all

Several towns in the USSR have fine circus buildings. This photograph shows the permanent circus building in Volgograd.

there is a strange feeling of having been here before for all of us; and as the clowns and pierrots, the ringmaster and the stilt-walkers, the gorgeous girls and ill-formed humans of both sexes, the noble beasts in their cages, during the march around the ring, open huge cavernous mouths to growl (or, perhaps it is merely to yawn?) there is a blare of trumpets, the sound effects are amplified, the band's march mood changes to that of exciting adventure-motifs – and then, erupting into the arena, come a number of Arab steeds in a daredevil race, or a team of modern motor-cyclists if the circus is trying to be trendy; more likely though it's a return to the past, to the Roman arena, when the golden chariots vied with each other in the race to please the populace, and the Emperors; they who cheered, ate, howled for blood, drank their wines and were vomiting and letching all at the same time. There are certain authorities and 'experts' on the circus as it exists in our own day who refuse to acknowledge the modern circus's similarity to its ancient past. They write learned works and reject the thesis, because the Roman show was more brutal, depraved and degrading, that it can have its roots still in the past. But we cannot doubt that its appeal in the first two or three centuries of the Christian era was comparable with, if not similar to that of, the modern circus. And in no detail were the two more alike than in the start of the circus in the capitals of the world when the lights change, the trumpets blare, the galloping hooves, the straining riders or drivers crouch behind their charges and smite their steeds with whips and shouts of encouragement as the crowd settles down to another exhibition of skill and daring; they are all 'Ben Hurs', frantically urging on their mounts to win.

Whereas the tenting circus that takes in the provincial town (the village green, the moor, park, river towpath or heath, with a circus parade that marches through the streets with clowns on stilts and circus band, freaks and trapeze artists, and animal trainers) reminds one of the past with its string of wild animals and performing men, it is now brought in by lorry. Its bigger counterparts from the Continent (where the circus has never lost its popularity) or the United States usually travel by train. Naturally, any transportations made by the Barnum and Bailey type circus in the U.S. go by its own trains, owned for this purpose alone.

When the circus approaches, the crowds gather, wagon are positioned, the tentmaster, stableboys and studgrooms directing where they're to go; then all the performers as well as the tent management on the male side chip in to help in erecting the Big Top. Its site decided upon, it only remains for the stakedrivers to start work. Soon they start swinging arms and in turn, with an unending rhythm, each stake driver drops the mallet he's wielding on to his stake. Only grooms and prop men are excluded from the compulsory job, because it's their job to erect the dressing tents and stabling arrangements. Soon, in good weather and on soft surfaces, during which time the poles have been unloaded and guyed, the canvas gets spread, lacing proceeds, all is prepared for the erection and our tentmaster yells his last command. His crew hauls on

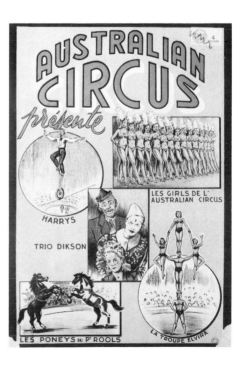

the ropes and the vast canvas goes into position. This becomes the neck of the tent. The poles – side and quarter – are there: the Big Top stands erect at last. If conditions are fair then the work has not taken much more than an hour; if bad it could take between three and four times this while. Breakfast for the animals and tent crew proceeds before returning for the tentmen to unload. All follows by rote: seat-building, ring-making, turf-picking to provide horses with firm foothold, sprinkling of sawdust. The artists meanwhile fix trapezes and high wires for their acts. The electrical equipment grinds into place, up goes the showfront, too, with its thousands of small bulbs to illuminate the entrance to the circus. Inside the Big Top a shadowy figure is seen now only through the light that comes through the canvas itself; if a dull day outside it is dark inside, but if bright then the reflection makes for the sight of a bare tent. Nothing more now until the lights come on to greet first audience and finally, once more for them, the performers. It is strange, brooding, expectant, and somehow quite like nothing else in the world: the Back-of-the-Big-Top life that attracts, before consuming, with a fatal fascination all who become its captives. The cult of the circus has not diminished with the times and if the most voluble of its adherents are not today quoted so fully and frequently as in the past, then that is maybe because there are so many competitors in the media. Always there is practice; 'perfection' – which is what all the master showmen and their artists have sought – is impossible to achieve. That, at any rate, is the conviction of all circus folk with whom we have talked. No theory here about this. Practice, work and practice, always striving towards that unattainable perfection. We once enquired of a world famous star practising between shows at Harringay why he was practising at this moment rather than resting when we had seen him practise the same routine as he was now working at for the three previous hours nonstop. We queried whether it was possible to attain further perfection, to which he replied, 'There is always *something* to be achieved'. For such performers, perfection is forever elusive; a non-existent word in a world where hopes are rarely, if ever, fulfilled. Circus rehearsals when we watch them show something happening all the time: acrobats warm up, trapeze artistes stretch to get ready for their most energetic routines, lesser fry on ropes, bar and wire balance gingerly. Horses trot and drill with sameness over and over again; their trainers driving

'routines' into their lovely skulls. Oddest of all are the clowns, not only because when going through their paces they have no childish laughter to encourage their efforts to be funny, but by their weird look (not so funny!) when they are out of costume and clad only in old bags and sweaters.

Divorce in circus life is more unusual than the deformed performer. They take their partners, these circus folk, for better or for worse, in sickness or in health or in death, and they enforce rigid rules regarding the sexual members of the 'team'. Perhaps the

A sea-lions' pop group at Bertram Mills Circus.

172

circus is not only less permissive than the big town or the village in which it plays or passes through but, what is more to the point, it is less inhibited also. Often the mates marry because they have much in common as partners and even if they aren't in love they make each other happy. Apart from the mishaps and the tragic endings of clowns fewer melodramatic problems present themselves in the circus than they do outside it.

One great admirer of circus people, the painter Dame Laura Knight, wrote this:

> I have often tried to analyse the circus appeal. It is the display of indomitable courage that one sees and admires, an admiration inherent in the human race. Gravitation is defied – the impossible is possible. I heard an acrobat say once: 'No matter what we come to, we have lived. I was king of the earth when I was young, the laws that governed other people did not govern me, I could do anything. I clawed my way through the air back to the net once when I missed my grip on the flying trapeze.'
>
> It is the feeling of defiance for the laws of nature that makes the circus people a race apart; they are one, although gathered from all races. I never felt a stranger among them; their acceptance of me as one of themselves has always seemed a miracle for usually, like fisher people, they are difficult to know intimately. Circus performers are the hardest working, the cleanest living people I have met, with a pride in their bodies, an ideal of attainment and an infinite capacity for endurance.

In Russia every big city has a state circus. There are different styles for different countries but the most marked contrast between the rest of the world and Russia is that circus there is an art form: in the words of Clem Butson, arguably Great Britain's best circus producer, one whose staging of the Blackpool Tower Circus and both the Tom Arnold and Moscow State Circuses, during the fifties and sixties in London made him well known: 'You can't "make" a circus artist. It's got to be inbred . . . In Moscow they have a school where only apt pupils are encouraged to train as tightrope walkers, trainers, trapeze artists, clowns and all the rest of it. Then they graduate, e.g. the clowns alone have a full-time curriculum. The Russian method of training is not only to extract the best of a performer's talent, but, as with ballet, the Circus over there believes in the indoctrination of self-discipline.'

The cycling chimpanzee Vanya and Gosha the bear from the Moscow State Circus.

The Krone Circus of Munich is considered by many experts to be the best organised in the world. Certainly, outside of the U.S.S.R. and United States, it is the largest: with more artists to perform, and a staff to service, as well as a bigger motorcade, than others encountered on the road; though the Sarasani Circus comes close behind.

The famed Hagenbeck Circus, founded at Hamburg in 1887, ended its career, spanning nearly seventy years, in 1953. However, it restarted in a new guise – albeit a traditional one for the family descendents of the original Hagenbecks – in 1954 when a training-centre for animal shows – no clowns, aerialists, jugglers – was started with a series of twice-daily performances on each day of the week, emanating from the Hagenbeck Zoo which had formed the basis of the original circus. At the time of writing one of the most popular (and comparatively most recent) developments has been the Dolphinarium, which was opened in 1970, for the specific purpose of training and 'showing' dolphins.

It is of some interest that the Hagenbecks were first involved in the menagerie market. Through successive generations of circus descendants down to the present great-grandchildren, they have now returned to the trade of their fathers. Many of the animals they train are sold to fellow circus owners still running their shows; others are used in their own all-animal shows that only occupy some half hour each performance. All the glitter and the spangles of traditional circus have been austerely expunged from the zoo that lacks the fun and gaiety and, some may think, the unique talent that made the name Hagenbeck renowned throughout the world in the past; but they are doing what perhaps the Germans do best in the ring, but doing it with less flourish and showmanship than of yore. Here is one circus existing in which the animal is paramount; the human ousted.

In some countries, such as Sweden, there is a law banning most traditional wild animals from appearing in circuses throughout the country. From 1960 the only ones allowed to

Below left The Flying Gaonas perform daring feats on the flying trapeze at a special performance at Ringling Brothers, Barnum and Bailey's Circus, celebrating 200 years of American circus.

Bottom right Annie and Minka Sinigalia in a spectacular aerial ballet at the Cirque d'Hiver.

An elephant at Chipperfield's Circus, performing in Cardiff.

perform in public have been those sections of the animal kingdom which are unlikely in the view of the zoologists to be humiliated and degraded by training: horses, asses, zebras, camels, llamas, goats, pigs, dogs, cats, sea-lions, doves, parrots. At the same time zoologists in other countries would claim that tricks are in any case not taught by cruelty but by mutual respect built up after a prolonged 'dialogue' between man and beast. Circus folk would agree with them and insist that they would expose any one in their ranks who was consistently cruel. Unfortunately journalism on the subject usually ends up with sterile and unhelpful exchanges of assertion and counter-assertion. Many travelling shows in Scandinavia have much to commend them, even though they never reach the level of talent and presentation achieved by their prototypes further south. Some of the small tenting shows have only their own large families to perform in them and do the whole show; and a good deal of what one sees is impromptu and off-the-cuff. They serve a useful purpose when they are 'workshops' for artists who have nowhere else to try out their talent, a new circus act, tricks, animal training performances; but they may lack style, taste and rehearsal. Circus folk in Sweden and other Scandinavian countries where there are restrictions on the use of performing animals are hopeful of the State helping with the subsidising of a circus-school based on the lines so successfully initiated by the U.S.S.R. So-called circus schools have been run in France and the U.S. but they remain at a recreational level.

While European circuses cannot be compared with the lavish Ringling Brothers units which tour from Florida, and are theatrical extravaganza based on circus, they can be compared with the many American tenting circuses which are less good than the best of the European: Circus Knie in Switzerland, the Orfei circuses in Italy, Castillia in Spain, Bouglione in France and Fossett's and Chipperfield's in Great Britain. In addition Australia and South Africa can boast a history of circus in their countries lasting almost a hundred years and involving some colourful characters.

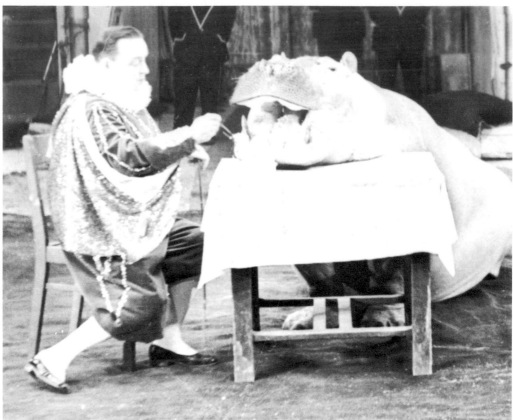

Meanwhile from Las Vegas comes a depressing story about a new pleasure palace called 'Circus Circus'. Here a resident circus company performs three times a day above the gamblers who remain indifferent to the show – unless an act is so dangerous they can bet on it. A contrast to this, and perhaps the most hopeful sign for the future, can be found in the smallest country in the world. Because of increasing difficulties encountered by circuses in France, the Prince of Monaco made strenuous efforts to save the circus from becoming extinct in his own Principality. That it has survived so well up to now is largely due to Prince Rainier's decision to hold an authentic International Circus Festival annually in Monaco; he presided himself over the organising committee which was formed to deal with the formidable task of enlisting the very best numbers and acts at an international level: in this way an entirely different programme was devised and produced for each evening performance of the festival. So far two annual circuses, lasting each for the best part of the week in the season, have stimulated enormous public interest, and circuses in America, Mexico, France, England, Spain and from behind the Iron Curtain have sent their most notable acts. The Prince's personal enthusiasm has managed to communicate itself to the audiences who have descended upon Monaco from all parts of the world. It is as though ordinary folk have become imbued with a feeling that circus as a noble art must not be allowed to die and that if 'His Serene Highness' can himself lead the way, in helping to preserve such an art form and livelihood for so many artists and showmen, then it is up to them to respond.

There have been many firm associations formed since the First Festival International du Cirque de Monte Carlo was launched on 26 December 1974, to be repeated on the same date in the following year; and the warmth and hospitality shown by the Rainiers towards circus folk was never more strikingly shown as when the ancient clown, Zozo, was entertained at the Royal Palace and encouraged to fulfil his desire to make a return to the sawdust ring and make people laugh again. For four nights Zozo was part of the show – the world's oldest clown performing in the world's youngest circus – by Royal Command. Similarly Gilbert Houcke, the once famous animal trainer, now paralysed as a result of a stroke, was invited to stay as a guest of Prince Rainier for the circus season, together with another aged animal trainer of renown, Alfred Court, who was honoured by the special award of a Gold Trophy for his services to the circus. Their presence brought tears of joy to the eyes of many, delighted to see their work honoured. Memories of past great circuses, when they were in their prime, were recalled and since the Cirque du Monte Carlo has been running so successfully, nostalgia has been much in evidence and blended with carefree fun. The Rainier

Above right A hippopotamus performs with the Moscow State Circus at Olympia.

Above Lou Jacobs, the American clown.

patronage has been a practical matter, for not only have these International Circus Festivals been televised, but the manner, style and talent employed in presentation have all brought new blood into the veins of a popular art which to Rainier is noble. A devoted addict, he redoubles his efforts each year – his hopes and ambitions for his self-imposed task and hobby are selfless. He wishes to share with the old and young – as he told the present authors in a letter recently – 'the pleasure, admiration, fear or laughter, whether adults or not, in a common love for the Circus Show.'

We went to the land of the circus and watched them at play. They never seemed to work. We saw them and remembered. We recalled the great and small shows both in England and abroad when we viewed the beasts and humans in action. The masters of the sawdust ring excited us by the wonder of it all and thrilled us with the miracles accomplished before our eyes; at the vision of hundreds of threads in a kaleidoscope that emerges into a pattern of superb execution. We try to imagine in vain a world that could ever be deprived of Circus; a source of excitement, so funny, so skilful, so daring, that its industry, courage and dedication have been taken for granted. We pity a world denied sight of Codona, the Wallendas, Popov, Barbette, those Liberty Horses and all the rest of the great cast of players, athletes, showmen from every place in the world. As children we loved going to see them – and now remaining children we still love the outing. For each act had and has a special fascination for all of us irrespective of age, condition, strata in society, temperament and taste and we adored every moment of the contrasted, that marvellously varied, programme: grunting and hooting sea-lions, performing dogs, snake-charmers, galloping horses thundering past, trick cyclists, jugglers, aerialists, acrobats, dashing ringmaster – the clowns, Ah, the clowns . . .

That the circus continues to be multi-national and still popular in these years during which the politics of nations often fail in understanding is shown by a circus programme dated August Bank Holiday, 1975.

Above The Shanghai Circus appears in Paris. Many of their acts are based on traditional Chinese folklore.

Left The King Charles Troupe of one-wheeled trick cyclists.

THE BLACKPOOL TOWER CIRCUS

presents a spectacular ring full of thrills, skills
and comedy in Circus Fantastic 75.
Ringmaster Norman Barrett introduces:
Britain's only woman trainer of wild animals:
the glamorous Mary Chipperfield with her group
of tigers, leopard and lions.
The world-renowned musical clown
Charlie Cairoli and Company.
From the *Czechoslovakian* State Circus
The 'cyclobatic' Five Bertinis.
Big and Little
the Shire and the Shetland
and the Pony and Monkey Derby.
The fantastic Kris Kremo
Switzerland's juggling genius.
South Africa's double trapeze
sensation The Marilee Flyers.
The Tower Circus Fountain Finals
with the Skating Rolwoods.

The crowds who hurried to witness these spectacles in Blackpool may have been less vociferous and more critical than those who made their way to the slopes overlooking the Roman Circus Maximus, may have considered themselves more sophisticated and have argued more knowingly, but we doubt if they felt any less enthusiasm for the Art of the Circus. The Romans came from the warrens and slums of a great capital; the others from the British Isles mostly and the Lancashire milltowns in 'Wakes' Week'. Blackpool, unlike Rome, is a provincial and overcrowded holiday resort, but both were polyglot and inter-racial and both assessed the skills of highly-trained performers.

In this, too, lies the primary difference between audiences of the circus ring and those of the theatre. From the circus we demand wonders, incredible feats and monstrously exaggerated humour. From the theatre stalls we expect realism and the more we can believe in the words spoken and the gestures made, the more we applaud. Yet we preserve scepticism about the man who can leap higher than a house-top and balance footballs on his fingers. 'It must be a trick', we say, settling back in our seat, as though 'trickery' accounted for all the charms and long-practised arts we had witnessed. 'It must be a trick,' we repeat, when the wire-walker risks his life without a net under him, three hundred feet up beneath the tent-top. If so, we are missing many aspects of circus art, and above all the infinite patience and practice which goes to perfecting everything from acrobatics and juggling to training an animal, wild or domesticated, who enchants the crowd for a fleeting minute of circus time.

But there are others, and we are many, who have disciplined ourselves to recognise the genuinely superior among performers in the ring, human and ferine, who know that a 'trick' has cost years of patient training and practice though it appears to be tossed off with an almost impatient shrug, who can compare the nonchalance of this or that wire-walker with the heroes of Astley's or Ringlings' in another century or a distant place, performed by people of different nations. To us, and those who share our zeal, the circus is not just an entertainment, but in the parlance of today 'a way of life'; not only something to go to see but something we imagine in all its byegone perfections and life-and-death challenges. Many recognize that the two necessities of life have not changed from Juvenal's time to our own; *panis et circenses* – 'bread and circuses' – to fill our stomachs and call forth our wonder.

Circus is steeped in the past for the reasons outlined in earlier chapters. Its traditions, its folk, its sense of adventure and daredevil thrills, are all part of that formation of a thin line stretching from Greece and Rome down to the present. But it would be idle to pretend – in order to maintain this thesis intact – that the circus has not kept up with the times both in presentation and equipment. And *world* circus is not dying, whatever many people may think. There are today more shows than ever, and despite the demise caused by there being no permanent 'homes' for seasonal circuses in London itself, there will be, to offset this bleak fast, the fact that three more circuses are promised for 'the road' this summer. The sole obstacle liable to stop the growth of the homegrown product will be the shortage of artists and staff, for even now both are difficult to

Opposite Douglas Kossmeyer, the 'Ben Hur' of the circus, revives all the excitement of the races of Ancient Rome.

178

obtain. Circus life is a specialised one: the hours are long and arduous and the work involved is onerous. One also has to undertake a number of jobs apart from being an artist, such as driving vehicles, building and pulling the show's Big Top down, and generally helping those 'jossers', who aren't performers, in such tasks as 'seeing-the-house-in,' mending the canvas, repairing the clothes, and many other routine jobs they will be called upon to do during the day's circus labour.

'How did you like playing to the 'Wood Family',' said one clown to the other. The two old troupers were exchanging reminiscences and in the parlance of the circus the name meant just that – W.O.O.D. – or empty *wooden* seats or benches encircling the Big Top's ring. The second clown reflected that it had been the same, close on the last score of years now, and said: 'I can tell by the date book. And I'll bet the big uns are feeling the draught, too.' The clowns nodded to each other; agreeing with the conclusion but dissatisfied with the situation. Then the smaller of the two, the 'feed', the knockabout who looked most comical in the ring and saddest out of it, was smitten with a thought, and said: 'Look!' His companion, the tall and slim loony type, followed the direction of the finger that was pointing across the moor in the direction of hundreds of terraced Victorian villas, over each of which was a television aerial and a mast. 'Look at 'em,' said 'Joey' between clenched teeth, 'thousands of 'em, millions of 'em'. The two old clowns stared for some time digesting this simple statement of fact before the silence was broken; again by the little fellow who looked up suddenly at his 7ft-3in-in-his-socks companion. 'It's no good getting a job with other shows—they'll all go broke; even if they let you out of this contract because they've got nothing to pay us with, it won't be worth getting another job in a circus 'cos the circus's all ashed up just like the cinema.' The little 'Joey' stopped suddenly. Another silence. Then, finally, the big fellow looked down at his midget companion and said very softly: 'No it ain't like that, really. Yer see, we're NOT like the cinemas, or the television . . . He paused and then: 'No, WE can go to each town and bring them *live* entertainment.'

Opposite Dancing horses at Bertram Mills' Circus.

Following pages Richly caparisoned horses and elephants go through their paces.

Sunlight strikes the poster for the Greatest Show on Earth and spotlights play on the dazzling parade inside.

Excited children arrive at the Big Top, and clowns wearing carnival heads run on to entertain them at Billy Smart's Circus.

Below A team of sensational Arab horses circle the ring.

Circus Slang

ANTIPODIST
As the derivation indicates an upside-down man; a man who juggles with his feet while lying in a trinka (q.v.)

AUGUSTE
The man with a red nose and baggy suit who is always at the receiving end when water or custard pies are flying

BALLOON
Paper hoop through which a bareback rider, usually a girl, jumps

BAR-WALKER
Public-house tout

BENDER
A contortionist

BOUNDING ROPE ACT
The performer works on a thick slack rope which is attached to a spring which enables him to bounce the rope up and down

BULL
Elephant

BUNCE
Profit

CATS
Wild animals (tigers, lions, pumas, etc)

CLEM
Fight

CLOWN
The white-faced man in the spangled costume

CONSTRUCTION
A metal or wooden-framed 'tent' used by a few small continental circuses; in fact a portable building which takes about four days to erect and two to dismantle. Seldom seen now

CUSHION
Small sloping ramp used by some bareback riders to assist them when jumping up on to horses

DENARI
Money

DIDDY
Gypsy

DONA
Woman

FLASH
Smart, showy

FLATTIE
One of the public

FLIP-FLAP
Acrobatic movement

FLYING TRAPEZE ACT
Aerial act in which people (flyers) fly from one swinging trapeze bar to another or to the hands of a catcher.

GILLIE
One of the public

HIGH WIRE ACT
A wire-walking act done at a great height with or without a net. The phrase is often used incorrectly by journalists and others to describe any aerial act

JOEY
Clown—probably derived from Joey Grimaldi, the Victorian pantomime clown

JOHNNY SCAPAREY
Bolt

JONAH'S BAD LUCK
Wagons sticking in mud

JOSSER
Anyone outside circus business

KICKING SAWDUST
Tenting

KID SHOW
Freak show

LETTY
Lodgings

LIBERTIES
Ring-horses

LOT
The tober, or circus pitch

LUNGE
A safety device used to prevent performers falling and injuring themselves when learning or practising difficult tricks. Often referred to as a 'mechanic'

MISSING A TIP
Missing a trick

OMNEY
Man

PERCH ACT
One in which the under-man or bearer supports a long pole on his shoulder or forehead while a partner does tricks at the top

ROSINBACK
Trick-rider's horse

RUN-IN CLOWN
One who appears only between acts while props are being set or removed. Also referred to as a carpet clown

SHANDY-MAN
Electrician

STALLING
Missing a trick

STAR-BACKS
Expensive seats

STREET-WORKER
Kerb-hawker

SWAG
Prizes on booths

TRICK
Any feat performed by a circus artist or animal, there being no suggestion that trickery, as commonly understood, is involved

TRINKA
Upholstered cradle in which a performer lies when juggling with the feet

VOLTIGE
A rider or riders vaulting on to and off a horse

Previous page A dazzling moment at the 200th birthday celebration at Ringling Brothers, Barnum and Bailey's Circus.

Circus Music, Films and Plays

MUSIC
El Caballero
Entry of the Gladiators
Quality Plus
Sunnyland Waltzes
The Storming of El Caney
Pahjamah
Bull Trombone
Big Time Boogie
Royal Bridesmaid March
Pageant of Progress

FILMS

He Who Gets Slapped (Lon Chaney) 1925
Sally of the Sawdust (D. W. Griffiths) 1925; remade 1930
Variety 1925
Vaudeville (Emil Jannings) 1925
The Devil's Circus (Norma Shearer) 1926
The Circus (Chaplin) 1928
Circus Rookies 1928
Four Devils 1928
Laugh Clown Laugh (Lon Chaney) 1928
Trapeze (Germany) 1931; (USA) 1956
Freaks 1932
Charlie Chan at the Circus 1936
Circus (USSR) 1936
The Three Maxims (Burt Lancaster) 1936
At the Circus (Marx Brothers) 1939

You Can't Cheat an Honest Man (W. C. Fields) 1939
The Great Profile (John Barrymore) 1940
Dumbo (Disney) 1941
Road Show (Adolph Menjou) 1941
The Wagons Roll at Night 1941
Captive Wild Woman 1943
Tromba 1948
The Greatest Show on Earth (Cecil B. de Mille) 1952
Man on a Tightrope (Frederick March) 1953
Sawdust and Tinsel (Ingmar Bergman) 1953
Life is a Circus (Crazy Gang) 1954
Ring of Fear 1954
La Strada (Fellini) 1954
Three-Ring Circus (Martin & Lewis) 1954
Circus of Horrors 1959
Billy Rose's Jumbo 1962
A Tiger Walks 1963
Circus World 1964
The Clowns (Fellini) 1970

PLAYS

The Circus Girl (musical) Lionel Monckton 1896
Polly of the Circus Margaret Mayo 1907
He Who Gets Slapped Leonid Andreyev (USSR 1916) 1927
Caravan (Katerina Knie) Carl Zuckmayer 1932
Big Top (revue) Herbert Farjeon 1942
Top of the Ladder Tyrone Guthrie 1950
Stop the World, I Want to Get Off Anthony Newley 1961

Bibliography

Barnum P. T., Harris N.
Humbug: The Art of P.T. Barnum, 1973
Bostock E. H.
Menageries, Circuses and Theatres, 1927
Clement Howard
The Circus, Bigger and Better than Ever? 1974
Clarke John S.
Circus Parade, 1936
Coco the Clown (N. Polykov)
Behind My Greasepaint, 1950
Cody William, Croft-Cooke R., Meadmore W. S.
Buffalo Bill. The Legend, the man of Action, the Showman, 1952
Cooke Charles
Big Show, 1939
Croft-Cooke Rupert
The Circus Book, 1947
Croft-Cooke Rupert
The Circus Has No Home, 1940
The Sawdust Ring, 1951
Disher M. W.
The Greatest Show On Earth, 1937
Eipper Paul
Circus, Men, Beasts, and Joys of the Road, 1931
Fenner M. S. and W.
The Circus. Lure and Legend, 1970
Foster F.
Spangles and Sawdust, 1948
Friedlander Ludwig
Roman Life and Manners Under the Early Empire, 1965
Frost Thomas
Circus Life and Circus Celebrities, 1876
Gorham Maurice
Showmen and Suckers, 1951
Grock
King of the Clowns, 1957
Life's A Lark, 1931
Hagenbeck Lorenz
Animals are my Life, 1956
Henderson J. Y.
Circus Doctor, 1952
Hippisley-Coxe Antony
A Seat at the Circus, 1931
Hubler R.
The Cristiania. 1967
Jennison George
Animals for Show and Pleasure in Ancient Rome, 1937
Kennedy David
Entertainment, 1969
Kerr Alex
No Bars Between. Lion Trainer to Bertram Mills Circus, 1957

Knight Laura
Oil Paint and Grease Paint, 1941
Le Roux Hughues
Les Jeux du Cirque et La Vie Foraine, 1889
Lloyd James
My Circus Life, 1925
Lockhart & Bosworth
Grey Titan, 1938
MaeGregor-Morris Pamela
Spinners of the Big Top, 1960
Chipperfield's Circus, 1957
Manning-Sanders Ruth
The English Circus, 1952
Mannix Dan
Memoirs of a Sword Swallower, 1951
Mardon Michael
A Circus Year, 1961
May Earl Chapin
The Circus from Rome to Ringling, 1932
Proske Roman
My Turn Next, 1957
Rennert Jack
100 Years of Circus Posters, 1974
Reynolds Butch
Broken-Hearted Clown, 1954
Sanger Lord George
Seventy Years A Showman, 1926
Lukens John
The Sanger Story, 1956
Scott Raymond Toole
Circus and Allied Arts, 1958-1971
Seago Edward
Circus Company. Life on the Road with the Travelling Show, 1933
Sons of Sawdust, 1934
Smith Lady Eleanor
British Circus Life, 1948
Life's A Circus, 1939
Red Wagon, 1932
Tully Jim
Circus Parade, 1927
Tyrwhitt-Drake Sir G.
The English Circus and Fairground, 1947
Wallace I.
The Fabulous Showman, 1960
Wirth P.
A Lifetime with an Australian Circus, 1930
Wood Charles
Drawing at the Circus, 1953

List of Plates

Index

Acknowledgements

The authors would like to express their sincere thanks to the following for their generous co-operation and help in the preparation of this book: Edward Adamson, Miss Kathleen Albino, David J. Barnes, Peter Black, Miss Brigid Brophy, Clem Butson, Roger Cawley, Fleur Cowles, the Cox family, Muriel the Lady Dowding, Weston Drury, Miss Irene M. Heaton, Miss Barbara Hogan, Alan Hyman, David Jameson, Hans Keuls, Miss Rula Lenska, Miss Maybritt-Sundin, Cyril Mills, Jules Moore, Hobe Morrison, Paul Myers, Mr F. A. Normanton, His Serene Highness Prince Rainier of Monaco, Paul Rotha, George Shepherd and his staff, Mrs Diana Turner-Valdan, Cecil Wilson. A word of appreciation is due also to those friends, too numerous to mention, who have encouraged us with constructive suggestions concerning items that have been published on the subject since the turn of the century. Some of the proprietors and editors, with their publications, are beyond our felicitations; to those who survive we make our acknowledgements. And more than a word of appreciation to Miss Joan Miller, for her unfailing and sympathetic help, and to our typists, for their patient unravelling of our words. Needless to say, any failings in this book are our own and not those of our helpers: Chapters 1–5 are largely by Rupert Croft-Cooke and Chapters 6–7 by Peter Cotes.

In addition, the authors and publishers are indebted to the following individuals, libraries, museums, archives and organisations for permission to reproduce illustrations: Camera Press, 124, 132, 133, 141 top, 152 bottom, 163, 169 left, 171 top; Keystone, 112, 114, 116, 117, 119, 130, 134, 135, 136 top, 138, 140 top, 145, 148, 151, 152 top right, 156, 164, 169 right, 174 right, 177 top, 181, 182, 184; Zefa, 131, 152 top left, 162; El Bado Museum, Tunisia (photo, A.C. Cooper), 6, 10, 19, 22; by courtesy of Maeve Gilmore, half title, 161 top right and left; Bibliothèque Nationale, Paris, 7 (photo, Giraudon), 8 top (photo, Snark International), 37, 144 (photo, Giraudon); Snark International, 13, 38, 55 top and bottom left, 65 top left and bottom right, 78, 161 bottom right and left; British Museum, 8 bottom (photo, Snark International), 14 (photo, Mansell Collection), 16, 17 (photo, John R. Freeman & Co., Ltd.); Tarquinia Museum, (photo, A. C. Cooper Ltd.); Italian State Tourist Office, London, 10; Mansell Collection, 12, 15, 30 top, 31 top, 47, 48, 50, 60 bottom, 62, 64, 68, 80, 81, 110 right, 121; National Museum, Naples, 17 right (photo, Giraudon); Lyons, Musée de la Civilisation Gallo-Romaine, 18; Museo Nazionale, Rome (photo, Anderson-Giraudon), 25; Radio Times Hulton Picture Library, 27, 28, 29, 30 bottom, 32, 33, 34 top, 39, 40 top, 46, 52, 58 top, 59, 60 top, 63, 69, 70, 71, 76, 79 left, 82, 83, 84, 85 bottom, 88, 89 top, 90, 91, 92, 93, 100 left, 108, 109 bottom, 111 top and bottom right, 115, 118, 122, 123; Mary Evans Picture Library, 34 bottom, 36, 42, 61, 72; Guildhall Library, London (photo, A. C. Cooper Ltd.), 38, 39, 40 bottom, 41, 43, 44 left, 73, 89 bottom; Ullstein Bilderdienst, 31 bottom, 143 top; John Bignell, 44 right, 49; Circus World Museum, Baraboo, Wisconsin, back jacket, 53, 58 bottom, 66 bottom left and right, 67 bottom left, 74, 75, 79 right, 85 top, 99, 100, 101, 102, 103, 125, 159 right; Paris, Musée des Arts Decoratifs, 65 top right and bottom left; Museum of the City of New York, New York, 67 bottom right (photo, Scala); Victoria and Albert Museum, London, 77 top and bottom left (photo, A. C. Cooper Ltd.), 77 bottom right (photo, Tony Russell), 167; Hoblitzelle Theatre Arts Collection, University of Texas at Austin, 87, 98, 104, 105, 126, 128, 140 bottom left; Laing Art Gallery, Newcastle-upon-Tyne, 95; A. C. Cooper Ltd., 96; Paul de Cordon, 106, 107, 127, 136 bottom, 158; Florida State University, 129 top; Gerard Marinier, 109 top, 110 left, 111 left; Novosti, 113 top left, 153 bottom right, 154, 155, 170, 173 left, 176 right; Deutsches Plakat-Museum, 113 top right, bottom left and right; Popperfoto, 123 left, 139, 146, 149 bottom, 150 bottom, 157, 172, 179; Ringling Brothers, Barnum and Bailey Circus, front jacket, 129 bottom left and right, 137, 147, 150 top, 174 left, 176 left, 177 bottom, 183, 185; Barnaby's Picture Library, 140 bottom right, 173 right, 175, 180; Museum of Fine Arts, Boston, 165; Topix, 149 top; National Gallery of Art, Washington, 166; National Film Archive, 153 top left and right; 159 left, 167 bottom, 168; Art Institute of Chicago, 160; Musée des Arts et Traditions Populaires, Paris, 171 bottom.